THE DEVILS

by

JOHN WHITING

SAMUEL FRENCH

LONDON

NEW YORK TORONTO SYDNEY HOLLYWOOD

828 Whiting J

1 000 598021

THE DEVILS

Produced by the Governors of the Shakespeare Memorial Theatre, with the Stratford-on-Avon Company at The Aldwych Theatre, London, on the 20th February 1961, with the following cast of characters:

(in the order of their appearance)

MANNOURY, a surgeon	*Ian Holm*
ADAM, a chemist	*James Bree*
NINON, a young widow	*Yvonne Bonnamy*
JEAN D'ARMAGNAC, the Governor of Loudun	*Patrick Allen*
GUILLAUME DE CERISAY, the Chief Magistrate of Loudun	*Peter Jeffrey*
FATHER URBAIN GRANDIER, the Vicar of St Peter's Church	*Richard Johnson*
A SEWERMAN	*Clive Swift*
LOUIS TRINCANT, the Public Prosecutor	*P. G. Stephens*
DE LA ROCHEPOZAY, the Bishop of Poitiers	*Derek Godfrey*
FATHER RANGIER	*David Sumner*
FATHER BARRÉ	*Max Adrian*
PHILLIPE, Trincant's daughter	*Diana Rigg*
SISTER JEANNE OF THE ANGELS, Prioress of St Ursula's Convent	*Dorothy Tutin*
LOUIS THE THIRTEENTH, King of France	*Philip Voss*
CARDINAL RICHELIEU	*John Cater*
DELAUBARDEMONT, the King's special Commissioner to Loudun	*Patrick Wymark*
SISTER CLAIRE OF ST JOHN	*Stephanie Bidmead*
SISTER LOUISE OF JESUS	*Mavis Edwards*
SISTER GABRIELLE OF THE INCARNATION	*Patsy Byrne*
FATHER MIGNON	*Donald Layne-Smith*
PRINCE HENRI DE CONDÉ	*Derek Godfrey*
BONTEMPS, a gaoler	*Stephen Thorne*
FATHER AMBROSE	*Roy Dotrice*

CITIZENS, FOOTMEN, ACOLYTES, a DOCTOR, MONKS, SERVANTS, a CAPTAIN, NUNS, two CRIPPLE BOYS, LAY SISTERS, PEASANTS, SOLDIERS, a CLERK, PAGES, DRUMMER-BOYS, an OLD MAN

Directed by PETER WOOD

Setting by SEAN KENNY

The action of the Play passes in and near the town of Loudun, and briefly, at Paris, between the years 1623 and 1634

ACT I

SCENE—*The main setting, which stands throughout the play has a cyclorama backing. In front of the cyclorama there is a raised structure, referred to as "the bridge", four foot six inches high and about four feet above stage level, which runs the full width of the stage. Wide steps, C of the bridge, lead down to the main acting area C, which consists of a large hexagon rostrum one foot high. The areas down R and down L of this rostrum are used as required for small "interior scenes". Each is permanently equipped with a small bench, a stool and a table. Provided in the flies are suitable flats or cut-outs, which are lowered as required, representing the cloisters, the stained glass windows of the church, the grille for the prison cell and house pieces for the street scenes. A "cruciform" structure is lowered from the flies to give body to the interior scenes of the church, etc. At the opening of the play the clear open stage represents the streets of Loudun.*

Before the CURTAIN *rises, loud organ music, by Chaconne, is heard. This continues softly for some time after the play has commenced.*

When the CURTAIN *rises, the stage is in darkness. The* LIGHTS *come up on the whole setting. It is a bright sunny day. The organ music continues. A corpse is hanging from a gallows* L. *A* SEWERMAN *is working in a shallow drain down* C. *People are coming from St Peter's Church. They enter* R *on the bridge, cross and exit* L. *Among them are* MANNOURY, *a surgeon, and* ADAM, *a chemist.*

MANNOURY. Shall we go together?

ADAM. By all means. (*He moves down* C)

MANNOURY (*moving down* C) Don't catch my sleeve. He spoke as if he were God.

ADAM. Grandier?

MANNOURY. Grandier.

ADAM. Very rousing to the spirit.

MANNOURY. You think so? Hm.

ADAM. So small a town is lucky to have such a caretaker of souls. Did I say that as if I meant it?

MANNOURY. No. There are things, my dear Adam.

ADAM. Things, Mannoury?

(NINON, *a young widow, enters* R *on the bridge*)

MANNOURY. Don't gape. Things said and things done.

ADAM. By the priest? Yes, I've heard.

MANNOURY. Then see.

ADAM. With my own eyes.

(NINON *nods to Adam and Mannoury as she crosses and exits* L)

MANNOURY. I've attended her. Medically.
ADAM. Have you?
MANNOURY. It's not widowhood gives that contentment. That walk.

(*They move to the gallows*)

ADAM. It takes a visit.
MANNOURY. It does.
ADAM (*looking up at the corpse*) Hoo, he dangles.
MANNOURY. What idiot is this?
ADAM. They put him up last night.
MANNOURY. Compelling sight. What resides, Adam?
ADAM. I don't understand you.
MANNOURY. What's left, man? After that.
ADAM. Ah, you've something in your head.
MANNOURY. Has he? That's the point.

(ADAM *and* MANNOURY *exit down* L
JEAN D'ARMAGNAC, the Governor of Loudun and GUILLAUME DE CERISAY, *the Chief Magistrate, enter* R *on the bridge. They are followed by two* FOOTMEN. D'ARMAGNAC *and* DE CERISAY *cross to the centre of the bridge then come down the steps to* C. *The* FOOTMEN *remain on the bridge*)

D'ARMAGNAC. Grandier seems to have got it into his head that the forces of good are a kind of political party, needing a leader.
DE CERISAY. His mind's been running on such things.
D'ARMAGNAC. All the same—politics—the terms seem strange coming from a pulpit.
DE CERISAY. So does wit.
D'ARMAGNAC. Yes. I disgraced myself this morning. I laughed aloud. Is that more becoming to the Governor of the town than yawning his way through the sermon, as I used to do before Grandier came here? (*He pauses*) I think I'll send the carriage on. (*He nods to the Footmen, dismissing them*)

(*The* FOOTMEN *exit* L.
The organ music ceases)

(*He moves* L) Tell me——
DE CERISAY. Yes?
D'ARMAGNAC. —this is a small town. Can it contain a Father Grandier? That proud man. (*He sees the corpse, turns away and indicates down* L) Shall we go this way?

(D'ARMAGNAC *and* DE CERISAY *exit down* L. *All the people from the church have now gone. The stage is empty for a moment.*
FATHER URBAIN GRANDIER, *the Vicar of St Peter's Church enter* R *on the bridge and comes down the steps to* C. *As he does so, the* SEWERMAN *lifts a bucket of filth from the drain and splashes Grandier's gown*)

SEWERMAN. Sorry.

GRANDIER. It doesn't matter.

SEWERMAN. It's wrong, though. The muck of the poor shouldn't be spoiling the holy purple.

GRANDIER. No, my son.

SEWERMAN. Lovely day. Hot.

GRANDIER. Yes. How can you bear to work down there?

SEWERMAN. Well, I used to keep my mind on higher things.

GRANDIER. I'm very pleased to hear it. What were they?

SEWERMAN. My wife and my dinner.

GRANDIER. I see. But now . . . ?

SEWERMAN. There's not the need. I've grown used to the stink. Nobody can live forty-three years and not have it happen. (*He climbs out of the drain to* R *of Grandier*)

GRANDIER. You accept it.

SEWERMAN. I have to. I'm a man. A dirty, sinful man. And my job is the drains of the city. If you were a man, sir, and not a priest, perhaps I could make you understand.

GRANDIER. Try, even so.

SEWERMAN. Well, you come to see it this way. Every man is his own drain. He carries his main sewer with him. Gutters run about him to carry off the dirt . . .

GRANDIER (*moving* LC) They also carry the blood of life.

SEWERMAN. Mere plumbing. Elementary sanitation. Don't interrupt. And what makes a man happy? To eat, and set the drains awash. To sit in the sun and ferment the rubbish. To go home and find comfort in his wife's conduit. Then why should I feel ashamed or out of place down here?

GRANDIER (*moving* L *near the corpse*) Put in that way, I can see no reason at all. It must be a pleasure.

SEWERMAN (*moving* LC) It's clear, sir, that your precious juices will never flow here. (*He points to the corpse*) And that misguided creature has dripped through his toes all night.

GRANDIER. Don't mock the thing.

SEWERMAN. Sorry.

GRANDIER. He was a man. A young man. Eighteen years old. They brought him to kneel at the church door on his way here. He told me his sins.

SEWERMAN. What were they?

GRANDIER. Being alive.

SEWERMAN. Comprehensive.

GRANDIER. Heinous, it seems. Manhood led him into the power of the senses. With them he worshipped in total adoration a young girl. But he learnt too quickly. He learnt that only gold can decorate the naked body. And so he stole.

SEWERMAN. And so he hanged.

GRANDIER. He confessed something to me alone. It was not for God to hear. It was a man speaking to a man. He said that when he adorned the girl the metal looked colourless, valueless, against her golden skin. That was repentance. When will they take him down?

SEWERMAN. Tomorrow. When it's dark.

GRANDIER. See that it's done with some kind of decency.

(GRANDIER *exits down* L.

The SEWERMAN *kicks the manhole cover into position, picks up his bucket and spade and exits down* R.

The LIGHTING C *dims to night effect. The* LIGHTS *on the surrounding areas dim to* BLACK-OUT. *The corpse is flown out.*

DE CERISAY, LOUIS TRINCANT, *the Public Prosecutor*, and D'ARMAGNAC *enter* R. *With them are the* FOOTMEN *carrying lanterns.* TRINCANT *carries a sheaf of poems.* DE CERISAY *crosses to* LC. D'ARMAGNAC *goes to* RC *and* TRINCANT *stands between them. The* FOOTMEN *wait up* C)

D'ARMAGNAC. Provincial life, my dear Trincant.

TRINCANT. I see. You feel provincial life has a bad effect on the art of poetry?

D'ARMAGNAC. Ask de Cerisay.

DE CERISAY. Well, you and I, Trincant, as Public Prosecutor and Magistrate, are brought close to the ground by our work. I've always understood poetry to be an elevated art.

TRINCANT. I assure you that during composition I think the right thoughts. My mind, if I may put it this way, is filled with nobility.

DE CERISAY. Why don't you show this latest bunch of Latin epigrams to Grandier?

TRINCANT. The priest?

DE CERISAY. As a priest his secular senses are well-developed. Make a selection. Submit them. The man is a scholar.

TRINCANT. Very well. (*He crosses to* L *and turns*) I don't seek praise, but I'll do as you say: yes.

(TRINCANT *bows and exits down* L)

D'ARMAGNAC. Poor Trincant. He loves the muses but, alas, they don't seem to love him. I hope your suggestion about Grandier was not malicious.

DE CERISAY. Not at all, sir. As with any author, the greater Trincant's audience the less burden of doubt on his closer friends.

D'ARMAGNAC. Grandier came to see me this morning. I was having breakfast in the garden. He didn't know that I could observe him as he walked towards me. Vulnerable: smiling. He visibly breathed the air. He stopped to watch the peacocks. He fondled a rose as if it were the secret part of a woman. He laughed with the gardener's child. Then he composed himself and it was another man who sat down beside me and talked for an hour. When will this other man climb on his ladder of doubt and laughter?

(NINON *is heard off* R, *laughing*)

DE CERISAY. Probably to the highest offices of the Church.

D'ARMAGNAC. And the man I saw in the garden?

> (DE CERISAY *and* D'ARMAGNAC *shake hands.*
> D'ARMAGNAC *exits* R. *The* FOOTMEN *follow him off.*
> DE CERISAY *exits* L *as the* LIGHTS *on the area* C *dim to* BLACK-OUT.
> *The* LIGHTS *come up on the area down* R. NINON *enters down* R. *She carries a small bottle of scent.* GRANDIER *follows her on and crosses to the bench* R *buttoning his coat*)

NINON. Tell me.

GRANDIER. Now what do you need to be told? Words are playthings in our situation. Expect music from them, but not sense.

NINON. Don't laugh at me. I never understand. I'm not a clever woman.

GRANDIER. You're too humble, Ninon. It's a female vice. It will never do. (*He sits on the bench*) Ask your question.

NINON. Why do you come to me?

GRANDIER. That would be a good question if we were in your drawing-room. As it is . . .

NINON (*moving to him*) There are pretty young girls in the town.

GRANDIER. They didn't need consolation for the untimely death of their husband, the rich wine merchant. That was the reason for my first visit, remember. How many Tuesdays ago was it?

> (NINON *laughs*)

I asked you to believe that God loved you, and had you in His eternal care. That the bursting of your husband's heart at the dinner table, when his blood ran with his wholesale wine, was an act of love. That all things, however incomprehensible, are an act of love. But you couldn't bring yourself to believe any of this. Your soul is as tiny as your mind, Ninon, and you had to fall back on a most human gesture; you wept. Tears must be wiped away. How can that be done without a caress? (*He caresses her*)

NINON. I saw you that day just as a man.

> (GRANDIER *takes the scent, turns away and applies scent to his handkerchief*)

What's the matter?

GRANDIER. I wish words like that could still hurt me.

NINON. I've never seen you as anything but a man. Do you want to be more?

GRANDIER. Of course. Or less.

NINON. But how can you be a man of God without being a man?

GRANDIER. My dear child, you ask questions out of your time, and far beyond your experience. (*He rises*) Your mouth . . . (*He kisses her*)

NINON. You possess me.

GRANDIER. You've been a good little animal today. Let the thought of it comfort you. Be happy.

(GRANDIER *exits down* R.

NINON *slowly follows him off as the* LIGHTS *on the area down* R *dim to* BLACK-OUT. *The* LIGHTS *come up on the area down* L. MANNOURY *is seated on the bench studying a human head in a bucket.* ADAM *is at the table, working with a mortar and pestle*)

MANNOURY. This human head fills me with anticipation, my dear Adam.

ADAM. It's a common enough object.

MANNOURY. Every man wears one on his shoulders, certainly. But when a head comes into my hands, dissociated from the grosser parts of the body, I always feel an elevation of spirit. Think—this is the residence of reason.

ADAM. Indeed. Ah, yes. Very trying.

MANNOURY. Isn't it possible that one day in the most commonplace dissection I might find . . . ? (*He turns to Adam and groans*)

ADAM. Find what, Mannoury? Don't hesitate to tell me.

MANNOURY. I might stumble upon the very meaning of reason. Isn't it possible that the divinity of man, enclosed in an infinitesimal bag, might rest upon the point of my knife? I have dreamed of the moment. I have seen myself. I lift the particle, taken from the cerebellum and, Adam, I know.

ADAM. What do you know, Mannoury?

MANNOURY. Come, my dear friend, I am speaking in the most comprehensive sense. I know—everything. All—is revealed.

ADAM. God bless my soul.

MANNOURY (*rising*) Let's take this thing to your house. (*He covers the head with a napkin*) We'll spend the evening on it.

(ADAM *and* MANNOURY *cross to* C *as the* LIGHTS *on the area down* L *dim to* BLACK-OUT. *The* LIGHTS *come up on the area* C)

ADAM. Is Madam-who-shall-be-nameless delivered?

MANNOURY. Prematurely. The foetus was interesting. It had a tiny cap drawn over its head.

ADAM. Hardly surprising with all this talk about the coachman.

(GRANDIER *enters down* R)

MANNOURY. Look who's coming.

ADAM. Studied indifference, if you please.

GRANDIER (*crossing to* R *of Mannoury and Adam*) Good evening, Mr Surgeon.

MANNOURY. Good evening, sir.

GRANDIER. And Mr Chemist.

ADAM. Sir.

GRANDIER. It's been a fine day.

MANNOURY (*crossing to* RC) Yes.

GRANDIER (*intercepting Adam*) But now—rain, do you think?
ADAM. The sky is clear.
MANNOURY. It is.
GRANDIER. But it may cloud over before night.
ADAM. Indeed.
MANNOURY. Indeed, it may.
GRANDIER. Darken, you know. What have you got in that bucket?
MANNOURY. A man's head.
GRANDIER. A friend?
MANNOURY. A criminal.
ADAM. The body was taken down from the gallows last night.

GRANDIER (*after a pause*) I hope they didn't overcharge you, in the interest of science.
MANNOURY. Ninepence.
GRANDIER. Reasonable. A bargain. Let me see. (*He takes the bucket from Mannoury and looks in it*) Poor pickle.
ADAM. Yes. Mannoury and I have been discussing the human predicament with this relic as centrepiece.
GRANDIER. I'm sure you said some very interesting things.
ADAM. Well, Mannoury did observe that the seat of reason is situated here.
GRANDIER. How true! But you'll have said that, Adam.
ADAM. I did.
GRANDIER. And we mustn't forget looking down on this pudding that man's *fiddledeevinity* is what you may say only to the greater purpose of his—(*he yawns*) huhumba. (*He returns the bucket to Mannoury*)
ADAM. I beg your pardon.
GRANDIER. I quite agree. (*He crosses to* LC) I mustn't stay exchanging profundities with you, however much you may tempt me. So good-bye, Mr Surgeon and Mr Chemist.

(GRANDIER *exits* L)

MANNOURY. You fell into his trap, Adam. Never engage Mr Clever.
ADAM. He smelled of the widow woman. Filth.
MANNOURY. Of course. He's just come from her.
ADAM. After tickling himself in the confessional with the sins of young girls this morning . . .
MANNOURY. He consummates himself in the widow's bed this afternoon.
ADAM. And then comes and yawns in our faces.
MANNOURY. Tonight . . .
ADAM. Tonight he'll spend in some great house—D'Armagnac's, De Cerisay's. Fed, comforted and flattered by the laughter of women. What a . . .
MANNOURY. What a . . . I'm so sorry. What were you going to say?
ADAM. I was going to say—"What a life!"

MANNOURY. So was I.

ADAM. We're never asked to such places.

MANNOURY. I've thought of it often.

ADAM. How do you console yourself?

MANNOURY. By remembering that I'm an honest man doing an honest job.

ADAM. Is that enough?

MANNOURY. What do you mean?

ADAM (crossing to R) Come with me.

(ADAM and MANNOURY exit R as the LIGHTS on the area C dim to BLACK-OUT.

A stained glass window is lowered from the flies C and remains suspended some height from the floor. The LIGHTS come up on the area C shafts of light that strike through the stained glass.

GRANDIER enters up L, kneels C up stage of the window, facing front, and prays)

GRANDIER. Oh, my dear Father, it is the wish of your humble child to come to Your Grace. I speak in the weariness of thirty-five years. Years heavy with pride and ambition, love of women and love of self. Years scandalously marred by adornment and luxury, time taken up with being that nothing, a man. (He pauses) I prostrate myself before you now in ravaged humility of spirit. I ask you to look upon me with love. Show me a way. Or let a way be made. (He pauses) Oh, God, oh, my God, my God. Release me. Free me. These needs. Have mercy. Free me. Four o'clock of a Tuesday afternoon. Free me. (He cries out) Rex tremendae majestatis, qui salvandos salvas gratis, salva me, salva me, fons pietatis.

(A "Grand Amen" is heard from the organ as the LIGHTS on the window and GRANDIER dim to BLACK-OUT. The window is flown out. GRANDIER remains on his knees in the darkness up C. The LIGHTS come up on areas down C, down RC and down LC.

DE LA ROCHEPOZAY, the Bishop of Poitiers, is carried in R in a carrying chair borne by three MONKS. He is preceded by two ACOLYTES carrying an ecclesiastical banner, and followed by FATHER RANGIER, FATHER BARRÉ and other MONKS, Capuchins and Carmelites. The litter is set down C. A DOCTOR enters R and crosses to LC. The ACOLYTES, the other MONKS with RANGIER and BARRÉ group RC)

DE LA ROCHEPOZAY. I have been alone for many days, now. Shut in my room, fasting and at prayer. You will want to know if I have found some kind of grace. Perhaps, for I am filled with weariness and disgust at the folly and wickedness of mankind. Is this the beneficence of God, you may ask. It may well be. Let me tell you, as your bishop, the circumstances of this revelation. A priest of Loudun called "Grandier" wished to see me. He is my child, as you all are —my darling, and I would wish to love him. But his handkerchief was scented. If this man had struck me in the face it would have humiliated me less. The assault on my senses was so obscene that I was in a state of terror. Scent, for a man to whom the taste of water was like fire, and the sound of the birds in the garden like the screams of the damned. (*He pauses*)

(*The* Doctor *moves to De la Rochepozay and applies the smelling salts*)

I am very tired. (*He holds out his hands*) Take these rings from my fingers.

(*An* Acolyte *steps forward and removes the rings*)

Perhaps on your way here from your parishes a child smiled at you, or you were attracted by a flower, or the smell of new grass by the road. Did you think of these things with anything but pleasure? One of you may have lost your way and been directed by a stranger. Did you think of it as anything but kindness? Let me say this to you. There is no innocence, none! Suspect goodness in men, and reject kindness. For all vanities are an assertion of self, and the assertion of self in Man is the ascendance of the Devil. When that handkerchief was flourished in my face this morning I saw it as if in a vision. It became a mighty banner flung across the world, stinking, enveloping, overwhelming our beloved Church in shamelessness and lust. We are in peril. (*He pauses*) Take me away. Take me away.

(De la Rochepozay *is carried off* R *followed by the* Acolytes *and the* Doctor.

Barré, Rangier *and the* Monks *kneel as* De la Rochepozay *goes. The* Monks *rise and follow him off.* Barré *and* Rangier *remain*)

(*As he goes*) I say again. The assertion of self is the ascendancy of the Devil.

(Barré *moves down* C)

Rangier (*following Barré*) How are things in your part of the world?
Barré (*moving in*) I'm kept very busy.
Rangier (*following Barré*) Is he among you?
Barré. Incessantly.
Rangier. Can we name him?
Barré. If you want to. Satan.
Rangier. How is the struggle?
Barré. I shan't give up.
Rangier. You look tired.
Barré. It goes on day and night.
Rangier. Your spirit is shining.
Barré. Unbroken at any rate. But there's never a moment's peace over at Chinon now. (*He turns to exit* L, *then stops and turns to Rangier*) Only the other day I was conducting a marriage. Everything was going very well. I had before me, a young couple, ignorant,

I thought, but pure. It never entered my head that they were anything else. I'd reached the blessing, and was about to send them out to the world as man and wife when there was a disturbance at the west door. A cow had come into the church and was trying to force its way through the congregation. I knew at once, of course.

RANGIER. That it was he?

BARRÉ. Say it, Rangier, say it. (*He shouts*) It was Satan!

RANGIER. You're never taken in.

BARRÉ. Before I could act he had passed from the cow to the bride's mother, who fell to the ground in a kind of convulsion. There was the most dreadful confusion, of course, but I began exorcism at once. There's a couple that won't forget their wedding day in a hurry.

RANGIER. How did it end?

BARRÉ. The spirit screamed from the church like a great wind. A kind of black slime was found smeared on the girl's forehead. She said she'd fallen, but of course, I knew better. That's not all. Two days later the husband came to me and said he'd found himself quite unable to perform his necessary duty. The usual kind of spell, you know. I've now started investigations into the whole family.

RANGIER. This sort of thing must bring a lot of people to Chinon.

BARRÉ. No. They all flock to Loudun now. This Grandier person, who's upset the Bishop, is responsible for that. He touts for his place disgracefully. (*He moves* L) I must go.

RANGIER (*following Barre*) Anything interesting?

BARRÉ. I have to call at a farm. They say that something is speaking through the umbilicus of a child. The child herself is now in conversation with it, and I'm told the two voices have evolved a quite astonishing creed of profanation.

> (BARRÉ *exits* L.
> RANGIER *exits down* L.
> The LIGHTS *on the areas* C, RC *and* LC BLACK-OUT. *The* LIGHTS *come up on the area down* R.
> *A* SERVANT *enters down* R *carrying a sewing-basket, a chair and a sheaf of poems. He places the sewing-basket on the table, and the chair down* R. GRANDIER *rises from his knees, moves to the chair down* R, *sits and takes the sheaf of poems from the* SERVANT. TRINCANT *enters down* R.
> *The* SERVANT *exits* R)

TRINCANT. So good of you to call, Father Grandier.

GRANDIER. Not at all. I've brought back your poetry.

TRINCANT. So I see. D'Armagnac holds that any insufficiency must be put down to life in the provinces.

GRANDIER. You write them when you get back from the office.

TRINCANT. Every day.

GRANDIER. Amid the cooking smells.

TRINCANT. They drift up.

GRANDIER. And the clatter of family life.

TRINCANT. It intrudes.

GRANDIER. And so naturally you achieve—these.

TRINCANT. Put me out of my misery. I want an honest opinion.

GRANDIER. You're an important man in this town, Trincant. Men in public positions can't expect honesty.

TRINCANT. Speak to me as a poet not as Public Prosecutor.

GRANDIER. Very well. Your poetry . . .

(PHILLIPE TRINCANT, *Trincant's daughter, enters down* R)

TRINCANT (*to Phillipe*) What is it?

PHILLIPE. I want my sewing, Father.

TRINCANT. Please take it.

(GRANDIER *rises.* PHILLIPE *moves to the table*)

(*To Grandier*) This is my older daughter—Phillipe. What were you saying?

GRANDIER. I was about to say that your creations—these——

(PHILLIPE *picks up the sewing-basket and moves down* R)

—have great merit. They seem to be moral observations of a most uncommon kind.

TRINCANT. Really?

GRANDIER (*to Phillipe*) Don't you think so? (*He moves to Phillipe*) I'm speaking of your father's poetry.

TRINCANT. She's very ignorant about such things. Young girls, you know, dear me! Dancing, music and laughter. Finer things can go hang.

GRANDIER. She should be instructed.

TRINCANT. It's so difficult to find anyone suitable in this town.

GRANDIER (*to Phillipe*) Do you speak any Latin?

PHILLIPE. A little.

TRINCANT. Unless . . .

GRANDIER. That's not enough.

TRINCANT. Unless . . .

GRANDIER. It's an exact language. Makes it possible to say just what you mean. That's rare nowadays. Don't you agree?

PHILLIPE. Yes, it is.

TRINCANT (*moving to Grandier*) Unless you, Father Grandier, would undertake the instruction.

GRANDIER. Of your daughter?

TRINCANT. Yes.

GRANDIER. I'm a busy man.

TRINCANT. Just one day a week. A few hours in the appreciation of finer things. It could be done by conversation. Perhaps the reading of suitable Latin verse.

GRANDIER. Very well.

TRINCANT. Shall we say Tuesday?

GRANDIER. No. Not Tuesday. The next day.

(Phillipe *exits down* R.

Grandier *and* Trincant *exit* R *as the* Lights *on the area down* R *dim to* Black-Out. *The* Lights *come up on the area down* L. Adam *and* Mannoury *are in the pharmacy, beneath a stuffed crocodile and hanging bladders. Light is reflected through bottles on some shelves, which hold malformed creatures.* Adam *is sitting on the bench reading from some pieces of paper.* Mannoury *is pacing up and down* L)

Adam. At half past five on Tuesday he left the widow's house.

Mannoury. The man is a machine. Interesting, though. Can sexual response be conditioned by the clock?

Adam. At half past seven he was observed in public conversation with D'Armagnac. The subject is in doubt, although Grandier was seen to snigger twice. He dined alone, later than usual, at nine o'clock. A light burned in his room until after midnight.

Mannoury. I suppose it's possible. I say to a woman, "At four-thirty on Tuesday I shall arrive to pleasure you." I do so on the dot of some weeks. It no longer becomes necessary to say that I shall do so. Anticipation speaks for me. (*He sits on the stool*) Tuesday! Half past four. Usual physiological manifestations. Subject for treatise. Must think.

Adam (*referring to another piece of paper*) Discovered at dawn prostrate before altar. Great languor through the morning. A meal at a quarter past two. Sweetbreads in cream, followed by a rank cheese. Wine—three o'clock: entered Trincant's house for instruction of Trincant's daughter Phillipe.

Mannoury. Adam, you're a wit.

Adam. Am I, now?

Mannoury. Your inflexion on the word "instruction" was masterly.

Adam. Thank you.

Mannoury (*rising and moving to Adam*) But forgive me, my dear friend, if I ask you something. How do we go on? Your observations of Grandier's movements are a marvel. But these are the habits of any man. We shall never catch him on such evidence. (*He moves to the stool and sits*)

Adam. You must give me time, Mannoury. We shall never expose him on his habits, certainly. But lust is leading him by the nose. And lust must have a partner.

(*The* Lights *on the area down* L *dim to* Black-Out *and a spotlight comes up on the area* C. Adam *continues to speak*)

The widow, Ninon?

(Ninon, *in the dim light, is seen to enter down* L, *cross and exit down* R)

Phillipe Trincant?

(PHILLIPE, *in the dim light, is seen to enter down* R *carrying a book. She sits in the chair down* R *and reads*)

Another?

(SISTER JEANNE OF THE ANGELS, *the Prioress of St Ursula's Convent, enters* R *on the bridge, comes down the steps to* C *and kneels in the light of the spotlight. She is humpbacked*)

Who knows? But there will be a time. Patience.

JEANNE (*praying*) I dedicate myself humbly to Your service. You have made me, both in stature and in spirit, a little woman. And I have a small imagination, too. That is why, in Your infinite wisdom, You have given me this visible burden on my back to remind me day by day of what I must carry.

(LIGHTS *come up on the bridge*)

Oh, my dear Lord, I find it difficult to turn in my bed, and so in the small and desperate hours I am reminded of Your burden, the Cross, on the long road.

(*Several* NUNS *enter* R *on the bridge, cross slowly and exit* L)

You have brought meaning to my life by my appointment to this Ursaline house. I will try to guide the Sisters of this place. I will do my duty as I see it. (*She pauses*) Lord—Lord, I have had great difficulty with prayer ever since I was a little girl. I have longed for another and greater voice within me to praise You. By Your grace I have come young to this office. Have mercy on Your child. Let her aspire. Meanwhile, the floors shall be swept, the beds neatly made, and the pots kept clean. (*She pauses*)

(*The* LIGHTS *on the bridge dim to* BLACK-OUT)

Mercy. (*She pauses*) I will find a way. Yes, I will find a way to You. I shall come. You will enfold me in Your sacred arms. The blood will flow between us, uniting us. My innocence is Yours. (*She pauses. Precisely*) Please, God, take away my hump so that I can lie on my back without lolling my head. (*She pauses*) There is a way to be proud. May the light of Your eternal love . . . (*She whispers for a moment*) Amen.

(JEANNE *crosses herself, rises and exits* L *on the bridge. The spotlight fades. The* LIGHTS *come up on the area down* R *where* PHILLIPE *is sitting reading.*

GRANDIER *enters down* R. PHILLIPE *rises.* GRANDIER *sits in the chair.* PHILLIPE *stands beside him*)

PHILLIPE (*reading*) "*Foeda est in coitu et brevis voluptas, et taedet Veneris statis peractae.*"

GRANDIER. Translate as you go. Line by line.

PHILLIPE. "Pleasure in love is . . ."

GRANDIER. "Lust."
PHILLIPE. "Pleasure in lust is nasty and short, and sickness . . ."
GRANDIER. "Weariness."
PHILLIPE. "—and weariness follows on desire." (*She stops*)
GRANDIER. Go on.
PHILLIPE (*reading*) "*Non ergo ut pecudes libidinosse caeci protinus irruamus illuc nam langue scit amor peritque flamma.*"
GRANDIER. Prosaic, but fair. Give me the book. (*He takes the book from* PHILLIPE)

(PHILLIPE *moves slowly down* R)

(*He translates*)
        "But in everlasting leisure
        Like this, like this, lie still
        And kiss time away.
        No weariness and no shame,
        Now, then and shall be all pleasure.
        No end to it,
        But an eternal beginning."

(PHILLIPE *cries*)

(*He rises and moves to her*) My child, why are you crying?
PHILLIPE (*looking away*) I haven't been well.
GRANDIER. Do you find our little lessons too much for you?
PHILLIPE. No, no, I love . . . (*She breaks off—after a brief pause*) I enjoy them very much.
GRANDIER. Well, we've only had six. I thought they might go on, say, to the end of the year.
PHILLIPE. Of course. As long as you like.
GRANDIER. As long as *you* like, Phillipe. They're for your benefit.
PHILLIPE. I want very much to understand. All things.
GRANDIER. All things?
PHILLIPE. There are forces inside me as a woman which must be understood if they are to be resisted.
GRANDIER. What forces, Phillipe?
PHILLIPE. Inclinations . . . (*She hesitates*)
GRANDIER. Go on.
PHILLIPE. Inclinations towards sin.

(PHILLIPE *exits down* R. *The* LIGHTS *on the area down* R *dim to* BLACK-OUT.
The SERVANT *enters down* R, *removes the chair and exits with it.* GRANDIER *remains. The* LIGHTS *come up on the centre of the bridge.* LOUIS THE THIRTEENTH, *King of France, enters* L *on the bridge, and crosses to* C. *He carries a document.*
CARDINAL RICHELIEU *enters* R *on the bridge and crosses to* LOUIS. *The* LIGHTS *come up on* GRANDIER *down* R)

RICHELIEU. It is a simple matter to understand, Your Majesty. (*He looks at the document*) You have that paper upside down.

(LOUIS *reverses the document*)

The self-government of the small provincial towns of France must be brought to an end. The first step is to pull down all kinds of fortification.

(LOUIS *and* RICHELIEU *confer.*
D'ARMAGNAC *enters down* L *and speaks across to Grandier*)

D'ARMAGNAC (*to Grandier*) So. It's the turn of this city.
GRANDIER. Is everything to come down?
D'ARMAGNAC. That's what they want. It's a trick, of course. Whenever there's a so-called nationalist revival in this country it means one thing—somebody is trying to seize power at the absolute centre. This destruction of the fortresses has no real significance. It's a show of power, a device. Richelieu sits with the King of Paris. He whispers in his ear and out come the usual catch-phrases.
RICHELIEU (*to Louis*) If France is to determine her own destiny, she must be free within herself.
D'ARMAGNAC (*to Grandier*) Ignorant and crafty provincials like us cannot see beyond the city walls. So we have this order from the Cardinal to tear them down. Will it broaden our view?
RICHELIEU (*to Louis*) Such men as your friend D'Armagnac, sire, see with a little vision. Their loyalties are to their cities, not to France.
GRANDIER (*to D'Armagnac*) Have they given any reason for this order?
D'ARMAGNAC. When a man's intent on power, as Richelieu is, he can justify his actions with absurdities.
RICHELIEU (*to Louis*) Such fortifications provide opportunities for an uprising of the Protestants.
D'ARMAGNAC (*to Grandier*) Look. An old city. Those walls keep out more than the draught. Those towers are more than ornament. And from that fortress I have tried to administer my small sovereignty with reasonable wisdom. For I love the place.
GRANDIER. We must refuse to destroy it.
D'ARMAGNAC. We? I have—which means we can expect a man from Paris just as soon as he can get here.
GRANDIER. Let me help you in this matter, sir.
D'ARMAGNAC (*crossing to Grandier*) Do you mean it? There is a churchman beside the King in Paris. As another beside me here, do you also want to use this device to further your own ends?
GRANDIER. Conflict attracts me, sir. Resistance compels me.
D'ARMAGNAC. They can destroy you.
GRANDIER. I am weak. Yes, it's true. But equal power cannot be conflict. It is negation. Peace. So let me help you with all the passion of my failure. (*He smiles*)

D'Armagnac. Don't smile. They can destroy you.

(D'Armagnac *exits* R.

The sound of a distant trumpet is heard. The Lights *come up on the area* c. De Laubardemont *enters down* L *and crosses to* c. *A* Captain *follows him on.* Richelieu *comes down from the bridge to* De Laubardemont)

Richelieu. D'Armagnac, the Governor of Loudun, has refused to obey the order. Go to the town. Speak to him. Find a way.

(De Laubardemont *kneels, kisses* Richelieu's *ring, rises and turns to go*)

Wait!

(De Laubardemont *stops and turns*)

There is a man. His name is Grandier. He is a priest. Yes, there is a man called Grandier. Remember that.

(De Laubardemont *and the* Captain *exit* L.
Grandier *exits down* R.
Louis *exits* R *on the bridge.* Richelieu *follows Louis off.*
The Lights *down* R *dim to* Black-Out. *The* Lights *on the bridge and up* c *come up to full.*
Sister Claire of St John, Sister Louise of Jesus, Sister Gabrielle of the Incarnation, *a* Lay Sister *and two crippled* Boys *enter* L *and play with a ball up* LC.
Jeanne *enters* L *and watches them play. When* Claire *has the ball, she sees Jeanne and stops playing*)

Jeanne (*moving* LC) We have suffered a great loss, Sisters. Canon Moussaut was a good old man.

(*The others cross themselves.* Claire *drops the ball. One of the* Boys *retrieves it*)

Claire. It is God's will.

Louise. God's will.

Jeanne. So we have been taught. (*She beckons to the* Nuns *and moves down* c)

(Gabrielle *moves down* R *of Jeanne.* Claire *moves to* L *of Jeanne and* Louise *moves to* L *of Claire. The* Lay Sister *takes the Boys up* c)

All the same, his death leaves us with a problem. We lack a director. The old man served this place well for many years, it's true, but the life of sinful children must go on. Penitents, we must have a Confessor.

Louise. Have you chosen, Mother?

Jeanne. God will choose.

Claire. We will pray.

Jeanne. Do so. There is a . . . (*She has a fit of coughing*)

(CLAIRE *moves to pat Jeanne's neck*)

JEANNE. Don't touch my back. (*She pauses with exhaustion*) There is a man. His name is Grandier. He is young. I have never seen him, but God has often put him in my thoughts lately. I mean to . . . (*She breaks off*)
CLAIRE (*after a pause*) What's the matter?
JEANNE (*staring unseeingly at Claire*) Claire?
CLAIRE. Why stare at me like that? Have I done something wrong?
JEANNE (*seeing Claire*) No, no. I mean to write to this good man and invite him to be our new Director. It is guidance, you understand. He has been put in my thoughts.
CLAIRE. Grandier?
JEANNE. Grandier.
CLAIRE. It is God's will.
LOUISE. God's will.
JEANNE (*with sudden harsh laughter*) I am tired to death. (*She pauses. Calmly*) Yes. It is a very excellent and practical solution. He can advise us on the method of education for the children. He will oversee our spiritual needs. (*She laughs harshly*) He can sort out these damned problems of theological progression which muddle me day after day. Yes, it will be a good appointment. Leave me alone.

(CLAIRE *goes to the two* BOYS *and ushers them off* L. LOUISE *and* GABRIELLE *collect parchment and ink, set it on a table down* RC. *The* LAY SISTER *sets a stool* R *of the table.*
LOUISE, GABRIELLE *and the* LAY SISTER *exit* L. JEANNE *moves to* L *of the table.* CLAIRE *is about to go*)

JEANNE (*calls*) Claire.
CLAIRE (*crossing to Jeanne*) Yes?
JEANNE. They say I have beautiful eyes. Is it true?
CLAIRE. Yes, Mother.
JEANNE. Too beautiful to close even in sleep, it seems. Go with the others.

(CLAIRE *exits* L.
(JEANNE *moves to* R *of the table and sits on the stool. All* LIGHTS *dim to* BLACK-OUT *except for a spotlight on Jeanne*)

(*To herself*) Remember, Jeanne? A summer morning, children playing. Boy and girl. Paper boats sail the pond. Sun shone so hot upon the head that day. Children crouched, staring at each other across the sheet of water. Was it love? Flick. A toad upon a slab. Croak. Boy, head to one side smiling, gentle voice whispering over the water, "Look. Speak to your brother, Jeanne. There. Green brother. Hop-hop. Speak to him, Jeanne." (*She laughs harshly. After a brief pause*) God, forgive my laughter. But You haven't given me much defence, have You?

(Church bells start to ring. The Lights *come up on the bridge. It is market day.* Citizens *and* Peasants *cross and recross the bridge, buying and selling.*

Grandier *enters* l *on the bridge. He is preceded by two* Acolytes *and by two* Monks. *He is in full canonicals, magnificent, golden, in the dying light of day. His tread is quick, confident and gay.* Jeanne *rises and cries out. The sound is not heard by the* Crowd, *but* Grandier *stops. He looks around him, into the faces of the crowd, wondering which man or woman could have been moved to such a cry of agony in the middle of such careless activity. He comes down the steps to* c, *looks round, then goes on to the bridge and exits* r *with the* Acolytes *and* Monks. Jeanne *sits and writes. A rapid angular hand, ornamented.* Adam *and* Mannoury *enter* l, *move to the steps* c *and sit. As they talk the* Citizens, *etc., exit* r *and* l *on the bridge. The* Light *on Jeanne dims to* Black-Out)

Mannoury. The first thing to do is to draw up some kind of document.

Adam. An accusation against Grandier.

Mannoury. Exactly. We know about his debauchery.

Adam. Profanity.

Mannoury. And impiety.

Adam. Is it enough?

Mannoury. It'll have to do.

Adam. For the time being.

Mannoury. We'll present the paper to the Bishop.

Adam. It must be properly done.

Mannoury. Of course. Framed in correct language, decent to handle . . .

Adam. Something's just occurred to me.

Mannoury. What?

Adam. What will the document say?

Mannoury. Say? *(He pauses)* We shall have to decide.

Adam. It's not important.

Mannoury *(rising)* No. Just the means. *(He goes on to the bridge)*

Adam *(rising and following Mannoury on to the bridge)* We must keep the end in sight.

Mannoury. Always.

*(*Mannoury *and* Adam *exit* r *on the bridge.*
The Lights *on the bridge dim to* Black-Out.
The church bells cease. The Lights *come up on the area down* l. *A small curtain is suspended as a confessional.*

Grandier *enters* l *and stands above the curtain.* Phillipe *enters down* l *and kneels below the curtain. They speak in whispers throughout)*

Grandier. When was your last confession, child?

Phillipe. A week ago, Father.

Grandier. What have you to tell me?

Phillipe. Father, I have sinned. I have suffered from pride.

GRANDIER. We must always be on guard.

PHILLIPE. I finished some needlework yesterday and I was pleased with myself.

GRANDIER. God allows us satisfaction in the work we do.

PHILLIPE. I have been in error through anger.

GRANDIER. Tell me.

PHILLIPE. My sister teased me. I wished her—elsewhere.

GRANDIER. You're absolved. Anything else? (*He pauses*) Come now, others are waiting.

PHILLIPE. I've had unclean thoughts.

GRANDIER. Of what nature?

PHILLIPE. About a man.

GRANDIER. My child . . .

PHILLIPE. In the early hours of the morning—my bedroom is suffocatingly hot—I've asked them to take away the velvet curtains —my thoughts fester—and yet they are so tender—my body— Father—my body—I wish to be touched.

GRANDIER. Have you tried to suppress these thoughts?

PHILLIPE. Yes.

GRANDIER. Are they an indulgence?

PHILLIPE. No. I have prayed.

GRANDIER. Do you wish to be saved 'from this? (*He pauses*) Answer, child.

PHILLIPE. No! I wish to take—no, possess—no, destroy me. I love you. Him. I love him.

(GRANDIER *removes his stole, kisses it, puts it on the table* L *and crosses to* C. PHILLIPE *rises and goes to Grandier. The* LIGHTS *come up on the area* C *and dim to* BLACK-OUT *on the area* L.

GRANDIER *and* PHILLIPE *stand facing each other for a few moments then exit* R. *The* LIGHTS *on the area* C *dim to* BLACK-OUT. *During the* BLACK-OUT *the Bishop's chair is set* C. *The* LIGHTS *come up on the area* C.

DE LA ROCHEPOZAY *enters* R, *crosses to his chair and sits. He holds a grubby document and is attended by his* DOCTOR.

ADAM *and* MANNOURY *enter* R *and kneel humbly* RC)

DE LA ROCHEPOZAY. I have considered this document you have presented against the priest Grandier. He is known to us as an impious and dangerous man. A few months ago we ourselves suffered insult and humiliation by his presence. But this is neither here nor there. (*He signs to Adam and Mannoury to rise*)

(ADAM *and* MANNOURY *rise*)

What is your complaint?

MANNOURY. We feel, my Lord Bishop, that the priest Grandier should be forbidden to exercise the secretarial function.

DE LA ROCHEPOZAY. What is your profession?

MANNOURY. I'm a surgeon.

De la Rochepozay. Would it amuse you if I came and instructed you in your business?

Mannoury. I'm always prepared to take advice.

De la Rochepozay. Don't talk like a fool. (*He pauses*) This grubby and ill-composed document tells us nothing we did not know about the man. Vague and yet somewhat hysterical accusations concerning lonely widows and amorous virgins are all that I can find here. I'm not prepared to conduct the affairs of this diocese on the level of a police court.

Adam (*quietly*) He has powerful friends.

De la Rochepozay. Stop whispering. What did you say?

Adam. Grandier is protected by his friends.

De la Rochepozay. What are their names?

Mannoury (*nudging Adam*) Go on.

Adam. D'Armagnac. De Cerisay. Others.

De la Rochepozay. I'll accept your reasonable intentions in coming here. Although—God knows—if there's anyone I distrust it's the good citizen going about his civic duty. His motive is usually hate or money. But I will not accept your opinions, your advice, nor, for a moment longer, your presence.

(Adam *and* Mannoury *bow and exit* l.

The Doctor *moves to De la Rochepozay and administers smelling salts*)

De la Rochepozay (*to the Doctor*) Those two probably spoke the truth, but they must not be allowed to think that they influence our judgement in any way. It is vital that the Church should be protected from the democratic principle that every man must have his say.

(De la Rochepozay *rises and exits* l.

The Doctor *follows him off.*

The Lights *on the area* c *dim to* Black-Out. *In the* Black-Out *the Bishop's chair is removed. Scenery representing cloisters is lowered from the flies* c. *The* Lights *come up on the areas* rc *and* c *for night effect.*

Jeanne *enters down* r *carrying a book of devotions. She sits* r *of the table* rc, *opens the book and reads. There is a pause.*

Claire *enters down* l *and crosses to* c. *She carries a letter*)

Claire. Mother. This was just delivered at the gate.

(Jeanne *puts the book on the table, rises, crosses to* Claire, *takes the letter, breaks the seal and reads it*)

Jeanne. He has refused.

Claire. Father Grandier?

Jeanne (*reading*) "My dear Sister. It is with great regret that I must refuse your invitation to become Director of your house. The pressing duties I have in the town would not allow me the time to devote my energies to the advantage of your sisterhood. I very much appreciate all you say of my qualities and . . . (*She tears the letter across and presses it to her body*) Thank you, Sister.

(CLAIRE *goes on to the bridge and exits* R. *The* LIGHTS *dim to* BLACK-OUT *except for a spotlight on* Jeanne)

What is this divine mystery? ". . . pressing duties in the town . . ." "This act of love . . ." Let me see. Let me see. (*She laughs*) I was about to address myself to God in this matter. (*She puts the letter in her belt*) Habit. Habit. It would never do. It must be to Man.

(*A dim* LIGHT *comes up revealing* GRANDIER *and* PHILLIPE *on the right end of the bridge*)

(*She whispers the name*) Grandier. (*She pauses*) You wake up. Dawn has broken over others before you. Look at the little grey window. Then turn. She lies beside you. The attitude is of prayer or the womb. Her mouth tastes of wine and the sea. Her skin is smooth and silky, rank with sweat. The native odours of her body have exhausted in the night the scents of day. (*She pauses*) Look down at her. What do you feel? Sadness? It must be sadness. You are a man. Ah, now she stretches her arms above her head. Are you not moved? This is not the sophistry of a whore, whatever you may pretend. She shifts her legs, entwines them, lays a finger on your lips and her mouth upon her finger. She whispers. Those words were taught. She only repeats the lesson. Such filth is love to her, and the speaking of it is an act of faith. (*She laughs suddenly*) What was that you did? Stretching out to clutch the falling bedclothes. Was it to cover your nakedness? Is there modesty here? (*She laughs, then pauses. In wonder*) How strange. Can you laugh too? That's something I didn't know. Pain, oblivion, unreason, mania. These I thought would be in your bed. But laughter . . . How young you both look. Quiet again. The girl is heavy in your arms. She yawned, and you have taken up the shudder of her body. You tremble in spite of yourself. Look, the sun is breaking up the mists in the fields. You're going to be engulfed by day. Take what you can. Let both take what they can. Now. Now! (*She weeps*) This frenzy, this ripping apart, this meat on a butcher's slab. Where are you? Love? Love? What are you? (*She falls to her knees*) Now. Now. Now. (*She rolls on to her back, convulsed*)

(GRANDIER *and* PHILLIPE *can no longer be seen*)

(*In a suffocating young voice*) Oh, my God . . . (*She half rises*) Is that it? Is that it?

(*The* LIGHTS BLACK-OUT.
JEANNE *exits* R *in the* BLACK-OUT.
The cloisters are flown and the table RC *is removed. The* LIGHTS *come up on the bridge and the area* C. *The sound of a distant trumpet is heard.*
DE CERISAY, D'ARMAGNAC, LAUBARDEMONT, *the* CAPTAIN *and*

two Soldiers *enter* L *on the bridge.* De Cerisay, D'Armagnac *and* Laubardemont *come down the steps to* C. *The* Captain *and* Soldiers *remain* C *of the bridge*)

D'Armagnac. Good morning, De Laubardemont. Have you thought over what I said yesterday?

Laubardemont. I'm sorry, D'Armagnac. It's not a question of compromise. I'm here as His Majesty's Special Commissioner, but I have no power to negotiate.

D'Armagnac. You know, Laubardemont, grown men in this country are getting a little tired of the Father Figures which keep arising, so we are told, for our own good, France may very well be looked on as a woman, and submissive, but she's not a baby.

Laubardemont. I'm inclined to agree with you. But I'm not here for argument. I simply brought a message.

D'Armagnac. An order. Pull down the fortifications.

Laubardemont. What answer may I take back?

D'Armagnac. That I still refuse.

Laubardemont. I have a curious feeling . . .

D'Armagnac. Fear?

Laubardemont. No, no. Just that you've been influenced in this decision. And that there is pressure behind your obstinacy.

D'Armagnac. ·The decision is entirely mine. As Governor of the town.

(Grandier *enters* L)

Do you know Father Grandier?

Laubardemont. I have heard of him.

D'Armagnac. Well, this is he.

Laubardemont. Ah, Father. Can't you bring your influence to bear on the Governor in this matter of demolition? As a man of peace I'm sure you want it brought about.

Grandier. As a man of peace, I do. As a man of principle, I'd prefer the city walls to remain standing.

Laubardemont. I see. Well, I seem to be alone in this. If you change your mind and I earnestly hope you will, I shall be in Loudun for a few days.

(Laubardemont *goes on to the bridge and exits* L. *The* Captain *and* Soldiers *follow him off*)

D'Armagnac (*looking after Laubardemont*) Look at him, Grandier.

Grandier. A funny little man.

D'Armagnac. My dear fellow, we are all romantics. We see our lives being changed by a winged messenger on a black horse. But more often than not, it turns out to be a shabby little man, who stumbles across our path.

(D'Armagnac, Grandier *and* De Cerisay *exit* R. *The* Lights Black-Out. *The scenery for the cloisters is lowered*

from the flies. Nuns *are heard singing "Deus in Adjutatorium". The* Lights *come up on the bridge and on the area* c.
    Jeanne *and* Father Mignon, *a foolish old man, enter* r *on the bridge. They come down the steps to* c. *Some* Nuns *enter* l *on the bridge, cross and exit* r)

Jeanne. We are all of us so happy, Father Mignon, that you've been able to accept. We shall look forward to having you as our Director for many years to come.
    Mignon. You're very kind, my child. You have a direct simplicity which an old man like myself finds very touching.
    Jeanne. There are many problems in a place like this. I shall need your advice and guidance.
    Mignon. Always at your disposal.
    Jeanne. For example, nearly all the Sisters here are young women. I think you'll agree that youth is more exposed to temptation than age.
    Mignon. That's so. I remember when I was a young man—how I used to . . .
    Jeanne. I have myself . . . (*She breaks off*)
    Mignon. What's that, my dear?
    Jeanne. I was about to say that I have myself recently suffered from visions of a diabolical nature.
    Mignon. In living close to God one becomes a natural prey to the Devil. I shouldn't worry about them too much.
    Jeanne (*crossing to* r) I can speak about this in the daytime. But at night . . .
    Mignon (*following Jeanne*) It is a well-known fact, my dear, that the spirit is at its weakest in the small hours.

    (*The* Lights *come up on the area down* r *and* Black-Out *on the area* c. *The stained glass windows are lowered from the flies and the cloisters flown*)

Jeanne. Yes. I managed to resist the vision. Several hours of prayer and I was myself again. But the visitation . . .
    Mignon. Visitation?
    Jeanne. The dead Canon Moussaut, our predecessor, came to me in the night. He stood at the foot of my bed.
    Mignon. But this was a visit of love, my child. Moussaut was a good old man. You were fond of him. Did he speak to you?
    Jeanne. Yes.
    Mignon. What did he say?
    Jeanne (*moving down* r) Filth.
    Mignon. What's that?
    Jeanne. He spoke filth. Dirt. Jeering, contemptuous, hurtful obscenity.
    Mignon. My beloved Sister—Father Moussaut?
    Jeanne. He was not in his own person.

Mignon. What do you mean?
Jeanne. He came to me as another. A different man.
Mignon. Did you recognize this man?
Jeanne. Yes.
Mignon. Who was it?

(Jeanne *whispers. There is a silence.*
Grandier enters r *on the bridge. Two* Acolytes, *carrying candles,*
enter l *on the bridge and meet Grandier. They all move down the steps to* c)

My dear, do you understand the seriousness of what you're saying?
Jeanne (*calmly*) Yes. Help me, Father.

(Jeanne *and* Mignon *kneel and cross themselves. The* Lights *on the*
areas down l *are dimmed. The* Lights *come up on the area* c. Grandier
preaches as from the pulpit. The Acolytes *stand down* r *and down* l *of*
Grandier)

Grandier. . . . for some lewd fellows go about the town and speak
against me. I know them.

(*The sound of a distant trumpet is heard.*
Laubardemont, *the* Captain *and two* Soldiers *enter* r *on the*
bridge and cross to c *of it*)

And you will know them when I say that Surgery and Chemistry
go hand in hand, vermination against the wall. They have borne
false witness. They spy. They sneak. They snigger.

(Adam *and* Mannoury *enter down* l *in the shadows*)

And the first sinful man was called Adam, and he begot murder.
Why do they pursue me? I am not sick; if they be here, in this holy
place, let them stand before me and declare their hatred, and give
the reason for it.

(Laubardemont, *the* Captain *and the* Soldiers *exit* l *on the*
bridge)

I am not afraid to speak openly of what they attempt to discover
secretly. If they be in this church, let them stand before me. (*He*
pauses) No, they're in some hole in the ground, scratching, so that
more venom may come to the surface, and infect us all; distilling
bile in retorts; revealing lust, envy and blight with the turn of a
scalpel. Oh, my dear children, I should not speak to you so from
this place. And I should not speak to you in bitterness as your pastor.
"Do they provoke me to anger?" said the Lord. "Do they not provoke themselves to the confusion of their own faces?"

(*The "Amen" is heard on the organ.* Grandier *crosses himself and*
exits r *on the bridge.*
The Acolytes *follow him off.*
Jeanne *and* Mignon *rise and exit down* r.)

The LIGHTS *on the areas* C *and* R *dim to* BLACK-OUT. *The window is flown. The* LIGHTS *come up on the area down* L. ADAM *and* MANNOURY *are in the pharmacy)*

ADAM. It's after ten o'clock. Would you believe it?
MANNOURY. Well, we have had a nice talk.
ADAM. Have we got anywhere?

(*There is a knocking off* L)

MANNOURY. Somebody at the door.
ADAM. Can't be.
MANNOURY. Is.

(ADAM *moves down* L. LAUBARDEMONT *enters down* L)

ADAM. No business. Shut.
LAUBARDEMONT (*moving past Adam*) My name is Jean de Martin, Baron de Laubardemont. I am His Majesty's Special Commissioner to Loudun.
MANNOURY. Can I help you?
LAUBARDEMONT. I hope so. I am visiting the town for a kind of investigation.
MANNOURY (*carefully*) We are both honest men.
LAUBARDEMONT. I know. That's why I'm here. I've always found in cases like this that there are perhaps two incorruptible men of the town. Usually close friends, professional men, middle-class backbone of the nation. Deep civic interest. Patriotic. Happily married. Managing to make ends meet in spite of taxation. Austere lives, but what have they like to be nice. Gentlemen, am I right?
ADAM. Quite correct.
LAUBARDEMONT. Good. (*He pauses*) I want you to tell me all you know about a man called Grandier. Father Grandier, of St Peter's Church.
ADAM. My dear Mannoury, at last!

(ADAM *leads* LAUBARDEMONT *to the stool, where he sits.* ADAM *and* MANNOURY *sit on the bench. A cock crows three times in the distance. The* LIGHTS *dim on the area* L *and come up on the area* C *for night effect.* GRANDIER *and* PHILLIPE *enter* R *and cross to* C *a "secluded place")*

PHILLIPE. I must go home now.
GRANDIER. Yes.

(PHILLIPE *moves* LC, *then stops and turns*)

PHILLIPE. I don't like walking through the streets at night.
GRANDIER. I wish I could come with you. I would like . . . Ah, words, words.
PHILLIPE. What is it?
GRANDIER. Come here.

(PHILLIPE *moves to* GRANDIER *and embraces him*)

(*Gently*) I want to tell you . . .

PHILLIPE. Yes?

GRANDIER. You know the love-making . . .

PHILLIPE. Yes.

GRANDIER. I want to tell you, Phillipe. Among the clothes dropped on the floor, the soiled linen, the instruction, the apparatus, the surgery—among all this there is a kiss of passion of the heart.

PHILLIPE. I know. It is love. Human love.

GRANDIER (*after a pause*) You understand it that way?

PHILLIPE. I think so.

GRANDIER. Do I love you?

PHILLIPE. I believe so.

GRANDIER. Then what comfort can I give you?

(*There is a pause.* PHILLIPE *moves away slightly*)

PHILLIPE. I am a simple person. I see the world and myself as I have been taught. I am deeply sinful, but my love of God has not deserted me. It is said by Man that those in our state should stand before God. I believe this to be right. And I would not be afraid to declare myself to Him with you beside me, even in our great transgression, for I believe Him to be good, wise and always merciful.

(*There is a silence*)

GRANDIER. You shame me.

(*The* LIGHTS *on the area* C *dim to* BLACK-OUT.

GRANDIER *exits* R.

PHILLIPE *exits down* R. *The* LIGHTS *come up on the area* L *where* ADAM, MANNOURY *and* LAUBARDEMONT *are in conversation.*

MIGNON *enters* L *carrying a parchment and quill*)

MIGNON. I couldn't get any more out of the Prioress. I can prove nothing. She may be just an hysterical woman.

ADAM. Does it matter?

MIGNON. I'd very much like you, as a surgeon, Mannoury, and you, Adam, as a chemist, to be there.

LAUBARDEMONT (*rising*) May I attend as a disinterested party?

MIGNON. Certainly. If this is a genuine case, the more the mer . . . (*He breaks off*) I've sent a message to Father Barre, at Chinon. He's our great local expert in these matters.

MANNOURY. I shall be only too happy to give you any medical advice, Father.

ADAM. And I'll comment on any chemical or biological manifestations.

MIGNON. She already complains of a spasmodic but acute swelling of the belly.

ADAM. Fascinating!

MANNOURY. Not unusual. Sense of false pregnancy. Known it before. Nothing to do with the Devil. Wind?

LAUBARDEMONT. Conjecture is useless. It'll soon be morning.

(*The* LIGHTS *on the area* L *dim to* BLACK-OUT.
LAUBARDEMONT, ADAM, MANNOURY *and* MIGNON *remain down*
L. *The* LIGHTS *come up on the area* R *for dawn effect.* JEANNE *enters* R, *kneels and crosses herself*)

JEANNE. Please, God, make me a good girl. Take care of my dear father and mother and look after my dog Captain, who loved me and didn't understand why I had to leave him behind all that time ago. (*She pauses*) Lord—Lord, I would like to make formal prayers to You, but I can only do that out of a book in the chapel. (*She pauses*) Love me. (*She pauses*) Love me. Amen.

(*The general lighting comes up to full for bright morning effect.* MAN-NOURY, ADAM, MIGNON *and* LAUBARDEMONT *move* C.
BARRÉ *enters* R *on the bridge and crosses to* C *of it.* JEANNE *rises and crosses to* C. *The others group around her*)

BARRÉ. Let me deal with this. (*He comes down the steps, hands his biretta to* MIGNON *and turns to Jeanne*) Good morning, Sister. Are you well?

JEANNE. I'm very well, thank you, Father.

BARRÉ. Excellent. Will you kneel down.

(JEANNE *kneels*)

(*He stands over Jeanne. With a sudden shout*) Are you there? Are you there? Come now, declare yourself. In the name of Our Lord Jesus Christ.

(JEANNE *suddenly throws back her head and peals of masculine laughter pour from her open, distorted mouth*)

JEANNE (*in a man's deep voice*) Here we are, and here we stay.

BARRÉ. One question.

JEANNE. Pooh!

BARRÉ. Don't be impudent. One question. How did you gain entry to this poor woman?

JEANNE (*still in a deep voice*) Good offices of a friend.

BARRÉ. His name?

JEANNE. Asmodee.

BARRÉ. That's *your* name. (*He kneels*) What is the name of your friend?

(JEANNE *sways on her knees. She gives inarticulate cries which gradually form themselves into the word*)

JEANNE (*in a whisper*) Grandier! (*She rises. Louder*) Grandier! (*She moves around* C, *shouting and pushing the others aside*) Grandier! *Grandier!* GRANDIER!

The LIGHTS BLACK-OUT *as—*

the CURTAIN *falls*

ACT II

When the CURTAIN *rises, the* LIGHTS *come up through the stained glass window* C *and the "Grand Amen" is heard on the organ.* GRANDIER *and* PHILLIPE *are kneeling* C, *facing front. It is night.*

GRANDIER. *Benedic—Domine, hunc annulum, quem nos in tuo nomine benedicimus—ut quae cum gestaverit, fidelitatem integram suo sponso tenens, in pace et voluntate tua permaneat, atque in mutua caritate semper vivat. Per Christum Dominum nostrum.*

PHILLIPE. Amen.

> (GRANDIER *takes a ring from his finger and holds it out*)

GRANDIER. With this ring I thee wed; this gold and silver I thee give; with my body I thee worship; and with all my worldly gifts I thee endow. (*He places the ring on Phillipe's thumb*) In the name of the Father—(*he transfers the ring to her second finger*) and of the Son—(*he transfers the ring to her third finger*) and of the Holy Ghost. (*He transfers the ring to her fourth finger*) Amen. (*He leaves the ring on Phillipe's fourth finger*) Confirma hoc, Deus, quod operatus es in nobis.

PHILLIPE. *A templo sancto tuo, quod est in Jerusalem.*

GRANDIER. *Kyrie eleison.*

PHILLIPE. *Christe eleison.*

GRANDIER. *Kyrie eleison.*

> (GRANDIER *and* PHILLIPE *cross themselves, rise and move down* R. *The* LIGHTS *through the windows dim to* BLACK-OUT *and* LIGHTS *come up down* C *for night effect. The windows are flown.* GRANDIER *and* PHILLIPE *move down* C)

PHILLIPE. We should step out into the sunlight. Bells should tell the world about us. It shouldn't be night. And as quiet as this. Dear God, my husband, kiss me.

> (*They kiss.*
> The SEWERMAN *enters down* L *carrying his bucket and spade and a cage with a bird in it*)

SEWERMAN. So it's done. I saw you go into the church.

GRANDIER. It's done. And well done.

PHILLIPE. Does your bird sing?

SEWERMAN. Not its purpose.

GRANDIER. Do you carry it for love?

SEWERMAN. An idea which would only occur to a good man. Or one careless with hope. Or one careless with hope. No, I carry the thing so that it may die, and I live. He's my saviour. Who's yours?

GRANDIER. You . . .
SEWERMAN. Blaspheme?
GRANDIER. Yes.
SEWERMAN. Sorry. (*He puts the cage on the ground* C) You know the pits at the edge of the town?

(PHILLIPE *goes to the cage and looks at the bird*)

Where even your beloved here sends in my buckets. Well, there are days when the place gives off poisons. So I always approach it with this creature on a pole before me. I lower it into dark places. His many predecessors have died down there. When this happens I know it's no place for me. So I let the drains run foul for a day or two, and I spend my time catching another victim to shut up here. You'll understand what I mean.
GRANDIER. I have put my trust in this child. She is not a victim.
SEWERMAN. Just as you say.
GRANDIER. Come now, even at this hopeless hour you must admit more passes between human beings than the actions which provide you and the laundry with a job.
SEWERMAN. I'm not arguing.
GRANDIER. There is a way of salvation through each other.
SEWERMAN. Are you trying to convince me?
GRANDIER. I'd like to.
SEWERMAN. What about yourself? Has the little ceremony in there done the trick?
GRANDIER. It has given me hope.
SEWERMAN. Hope of what?
GRANDIER. Hope of coming to God by a way of a fellow being. Hope that the path, which taken alone, in awful solitude, is a way of despair, can be enlightened by the love of a woman. I have come to believe that by this simple act of committal, which I have done with my heart, it may be possible to reach God by way of happiness.
SEWERMAN. What was that last word?
GRANDIER. "Happiness."
SEWERMAN (*after a pause*) I don't know what it means. You must have made it up for the occasion. (*He looks off* L) It's getting light.
PHILLIPE. I must go home. (*She crosses to* L)
SEWERMAN. Yes. They mustn't find the bed empty. On the other hand they mustn't find it too full.
PHILLIPE (*to Grandier*) Speak to me.
GRANDIER. I love you, Phillipe.

(PHILLIPE *exits up* L.
GRANDIER *moves up* RC, *turns and watches Phillipe go*)

SEWERMAN. Speaking of love, some very odd things are going on up at the convent.
GRANDIER. So I'm told.

SEWERMAN. It seems your name is being bandied about by the crazy ladies.

GRANDIER. We must pity them.

SEWERMAN. Will they pity you, that's the point?

GRANDIER. What do you mean? They're deluded.

SEWERMAN. What were you, a few minutes ago, with that girl?

GRANDIER. I was in my right mind, and I knew what I was doing. You may mock me, my son, if you wish. What seems to you a meaningless act, the marriage of an unmarriageable priest, has meaning for me. The lonely and the proud sometimes need to avail themselves of simple means. I, too, have made fun of the innocent before now. Your debasement has given you an unholy elevation. From your superior position be kind, be wise. Pity me. Pity me.

SEWERMAN. All right. (*He picks up the cage and crosses down* R) Let's hope the good women of St Ursula's will do the same.

(*The* SEWERMAN *exits down* R.
    GRANDIER *exits* R.
    The LIGHTS *dim to* BLACK-OUT. *The cloisters are dropped in from the flies. The* LIGHTS *come up on the area* C *for bright daylight effect.*
    JEANNE *runs on* L, *pursued by* RANGIER *and* MIGNON. RANGIER *has a large net.* BARRÉ *enters* R *attended by two* CARMELITE MONKS. *One* MONK *carries a small box containing a holy relic, and the other a container of holy water.* JEANNE *runs round* C, *meets* BARRÉ, *stops and backs down* C *and falls to the ground.* RANGIER *throws the net over her.* MIGNON *stands above Jeanne. The* MONK *with the holy water stands* R *of Mignon.* RANGIER *is* LC. BARRÉ *is* R *of Jeanne*)

BARRÉ. *Exerciso te, immundissime spiritus, omnis incursio adversarie, omne phantaema, omnis legio, in nomine Domini nostri Jesus Christi; eradicare et effugare ab hoc plasmate Dei.*

(MIGNON *removes the net and hands it to the* MONK, *then sprinkles holy water over* JEANNE. ASMODÉE, *in a deep voice, speaks through* JEANNE, *who rises to her knees*)

ASMODÉE. You gentlemen are wasting your time. You're soaking the lady, but you're not touching me.

BARRÉ (*to the Monk*) Give me the relic.

(*The* MONK *hands the box to Barré*)

BARRÉ (*he applies the box to Jeanne's back*) *Adjuro te, serpens antique, per judicem vivorum et mortuorum*——

ASMODÉE. Excuse me . . .

BARRÉ. —*per factorum tuum, per factorum mundi* . . .

ASMODÉE. I'm sorry to interrupt you.

BARRÉ. Well, what is it?

ASMODÉE. I don't understand a word you're saying. I'm a heathen devil. Latin—I suppose it is Latin—is a foreign language to me.

BARRÉ (*returning the relic to the Monk*) It is customary to carry out exorcism in Latin.

ASMODÉE. Hidebound, that's what you are.

(JEANNE *pulls* BARRÉ *slowly down by his arm on to his knees*)

Can't we continue our earlier conversation, which interested me so much, about the sexual activities of priests?

BARRÉ (*on his knees*) Certainly not.

ASMODÉE. Is it true that men of your parish——

(JEANNE *giggles insanely*)

—is it true that they . . . ? Bend low. Let me whisper.

(JEANNE *laughs*)

JEANNE (*turning to Rangier; in her own voice*) Oh, dear God, release this thing from me. (*She turns back to Barré*)

ASMODÉE. Be quiet, woman. You're interrupting a theological discussion.

JEANNE (*to Barré; in her own voice*) Father, help me! (*She collapses in Barré's arms*)

(MIGNON *kneels*)

BARRÉ. My dear child, I'm doing all I can. (*He rises, beckons to Rangier and moves slightly up* RC)

(RANGIER *crosses to Barré*)

BARRÉ (*to Rangier*) The wretch thinks I'm defeated.

RANGIER. You are.

BARRÉ (*to Rangier*) He seems at the moment to be lodged in the alimentary tract. Are Adam and Mannoury here?

RANGIER. They're waiting. (*He points*) In there.

(ADAM *and* MANNOURY *enter down* L. ADAM *carries a copper kettle with boiling water and wears a slightly bloodstained surgeon's apron.* MANNOURY *carries a copper bowl with dry ice, two napkins, and wears a clean surgeon's apron.* ADAM *pours water into Mannoury's bowl*)

BARRÉ. Ask them to get ready, will you? Consecrate the water, while you're about it.

(RANGIER *crosses to* MANNOURY, *who kneels and holds up the bowl.* RANGIER *consecrates the water*)

(*He turns to Jeanne*) My beloved Sister.

JEANNE. Yes?

BARRÉ. It must be extreme measures.

JEANNE. What do you mean, Father?

BARRÉ. The fiend must be forced from you. Forced.

JEANNE. But is there any way, besides exorcism?

(RANGIER *takes the bowl from Mannoury and exits* L. ADAM *follows him off.* MANNOURY *rises*)

BARRÉ. Haha! They say the Devil takes residence only in the innocent. It's true in this case, it seems.

(RANGIER *and* ADAM *re-enter* L. ADAM *stands with Mannoury,* RANGIER *crosses to Barré*)

Yes, child. There is another way. (*To Rangier*) My dear boy, you look quite pale. The use of such methods in our job distresses you. Wait till you've been at it as long as I have. Anyway, the Church must keep up with the times.

(MIGNON *rises and helps* BARRÉ *to raise Jeanne to her feet*)

BARRÉ. Come, my dear Sister. (*He leads Jeanne* L) Through that little door. There lies your salvation. She looks like a child, doesn't she? Touching, um? Come along now. Pretty, pretty. A few steps. Let the power of good propel you. Not much farther. There.

(JEANNE *sees Adam and Mannoury. She screams in* BARRÉ'S *grip*)

(*Powerful; confident*) Help me, Rangier.

(RANGIER *moves to Jeanne and* BARRÉ *helps to hold her*)

Do you hear me, Asmodée?
JEANNE. Mercy, mercy.
BARRÉ. Nonsense!
JEANNE. No, no. I didn't mean it.
BARRÉ. Too late, Asmodée. Do you expect mercy now, after your blasphemy and filth against Our Lord?
JEANNE. Father! Father Barré, it is I speaking to you now, Sister Jeanne of the Angels.
BARRÉ. Ah, Asmodée, you speak with many voices.

(JEANNE *bites* RANGIER'S *hand and he releases her*)

JEANNE. But it's I, Father. Beloved Mother of this dear convent, protector of little children . . .
BARRÉ. Silence, beast. Let's get her in there, Rangier. Are you ready, Adam?
ADAM. Quite ready.

(BARRÉ *and* RANGIER *carry the struggling* JEANNE *off* L.
ADAM *and* MANNOURY *follow them off.*
The MONKS *exit up* L.
MIGNON, *left alone, kneels* C *in prayer. The* LIGHTS BLACK-OUT.
A scream is heard from JEANNE *off* L. *It dissolves into sobs and laughter.*
The LIGHTS *come up on the area down* R. D'ARMAGNAC *and* DE CERISAY
enter down R. *A* SERVANT *follows them on, carrying a tray with a decanter*
of port and three glasses. He puts the tray on the bench R *and exits*)

De Cerisay. The devil, it seems, departed from the woman at two o'clock precisely.

D'Armagnac. What about the others?

De Cerisay. The Fathers are working on them now.

D'Armagnac. Same method?

De Cerisay. No. It seems that after the Prioress, more normal Methods of exorcism are proving successful. (*He pours two drinks and gives one to D'Armagnac*) A little holy water—applied externally—a few prayers, and the devils go.

D'Armagnac. Then we can hope for some peace.

De Cerisay. I don't know.

D'Armagnac. Can't you do something if it starts again? As magistrate. I'd say such goings-on constitute a civil disorder.

De Cerisay. I saw Barré and Rangier the other day and questioned the legality of their methods. Next time, the convent door was shut in my face, I put myself in a difficult position if I use force against the priests. They've asked me to be present at an interrogation of Sister Jeanne. I'm on my way there now.

(Grandier *enters down* R)

D'Armagnac. Ah, Father. (*He pours a drink for Grandier*) You know your name is constantly being mentioned in this affair. (*He hands the drink to Grandier*)

Grandier. Yes, sir.

D'Armagnac. Wouldn't it be a good thing to take steps to clear yourself?

De Cerisay. Have you offended this woman in some way?

Grandier. I don't know that's possible. I've never seen her.

De Cerisay. Then why has she chosen you as the devilish perpetrator?

Grandier. You look frightened, De Cerisay. Forgive me.

D'Armagnac. You're the one who should be frightened, Father. There was a case some years ago—I forget the man's name . . .

Grandier. I don't, poor devil. But he was ridiculous and obscure. Proper matter for sacrifice, that's all.

De Cerisay. D'Armagnac and I will give you any help we can, Father.

Grandier. Can't I talk either of you out of this? When I came here this morning I heard the stories on the streets—I laughed. I thought you'd be doing the same. (*He sits on the bench*) Is the possession genuine?

De Cerisay. Not from the evidence I have. As I say, I shall see the woman today. I'll let you know what happens, but you haven't answered my question. Why should it be you?

Grandier. Secluded women. They give themselves to God, but something remains which cries out to be given to Man. Imagine being awakened in the night by a quite innocent dream. A dream of your childhood, or of a friend not seen for many years, or even the vision of a good meal. Now, this is sin. And so you must take up your little whip and scourge your body. We call that discipline. But pain is sensuality, and in its vortex spin images of horror and lust. My beloved Sister in Jesus seems to have fixed her mind on me. There is no reason, De Cerisay. A dropped handkerchief, a scribbled note, a piece of gossip. Any of these things found in the desert of mind and body caused by continual prayer can bring hope. And with hope comes love. And, as we all know, with love comes hate. So I possess this woman. God help her in her terror and unhappiness. God help her. (*He puts his glass on the tray and rises*)

(JEANNE, *lying on a litter, is carried on* L *by* ADAM *and* MANNOURY. MIGNON, RANGIER *and* BARRÉ *follow them on. The litter is set* C.

A CLERK *enters with a small table, stool and writing materials, puts the table down up* RC *and sits at it.* DE CERISAY *and* D'ARMAGNAC *put their glasses on the tray*)

GRANDIER (*to D'Armagnac*) Now, sir, the business I called on. I've the new plans for your garden summer-house. Will you come and see them? I've revised and modified the frivolity of the design. As you wished.

(GRANDIER *and* D'ARMAGNAC *exit down* R.

The SERVANT *enters down* R, *collects the tray, etc., and exits.*

The LIGHTS BLACK-OUT *on the area down* R. DE CERISAY *moves* RC. *The* LIGHTS *come up on the area* C. RANGIER *and* BARRÉ *are up* R *of the litter.* MIGNON *is* L *of it.* ADAM *and* MANNOURY *are standing* RC. DE CERISAY *crosses to* MIGNON *and shakes hands with him*)

BARRÉ. Dear Sister in Christ, I must question you further.

(*The* CLERK *records the interrogation*)

JEANNE. Yes, Father.
BARRÉ. Do you remember the first time your thoughts were turned to these evil things?
JEANNE. Very well.
BARRÉ. Tell us.

(JEANNE *sits up*)

JEANNE. I was walking in the garden. I stopped. Lying at my feet was a stick of hawthorn. I was simply possessed by anger, for that very morning I'd had cause to admonish two of the Sisters for neglecting their duties in the garden. I picked up the unsightly thing in rage. It must have been thorned, for blood ran from my body. Seeing the blood, I was filled with tenderness.
RANGIER. But this revelation may have come from a very different source.
BARRÉ (*indicating the Clerk*) Is he getting this down?
JEANNE. There was another time.
BARRÉ. Tell us.

JEANNE. A day or two later. It was a beautiful morning. I'd had a night of dreamless sleep. On the threshold of my room lay a bunch of roses. I picked them up and tucked them into my belt. Suddenly, I was seized by a violent trembling in my right arm. And a great knowledge of love. This persisted throughout my orisons. I was unable to put my mind to anything. It was entirely filled with the representation of a man which had been deeply and inwardly impressed upon me.

BARRÉ. Do you know who sent these flowers?

JEANNE (*after a long pause; quietly*) Grandier. Grandier.

BARRÉ. What is his rank?

JEANNE. Priest.

BARRÉ. Of what church?

JEANNE. St Peter's.

(BARRÉ *stares in silence at De Cerisay*)

DE CERISAY (*quietly*) This is nothing.

BARRÉ (*turning to Jeanne*) We are unconvinced, my dear Sister. And if our conviction remains untouched I do not have to remind you that you face eternal damnation.

(JEANNE *suddenly throws herself face downwards on the litter, her head down stage. She grinds her teeth. The others draw back a little from her*)

(*With great urgency*) Speak! Speak!

JEANNE. It—was—night. Day's done.

BARRÉ. Yes?

JEANNE (*kneeling up*) I had tied back my hair and scrubbed my face. Back to childhood, eh? Poor Jeanne. Grown woman. Made for —for . . . (*She breaks off*)

BARRÉ. Go on.

JEANNE. He came to me.

BARRÉ. Name him.

JEANNE (*at once*) Grandier. Grandier! The beautiful, golden lion entered my room, smiling.

BARRÉ. Was he alone?

JEANNE. No. Six of his creatures were with him.

BARRÉ. Then?

JEANNE. He took me gently in his arms and carried me to the chapel. His creatures each took one of my beloved Sisters.

BARRÉ. What took place?

JEANNE (*smiling*) Oh, my dear Father, think of our little chapel, so simple, so unadorned. That night it was a place of luxury and scented heat. Let me tell you. It was full of laughter and music. There were velvets, silks, metals, and the wood wasn't scrubbed— no, not at all. Yes, and there was food. High animal flesh, and wine, heavy, like the fruit from the East. I'd read about it all. How we stuffed ourselves.

DE CERISAY. This is an innocent vision of hell.
BARRÉ. Ssh! (*To Jeanne*) Go on.
JEANNE. I forgot. We were beautifully dressed. I wore my clothes as if they were part of my body. Later, when I was naked, I fell among thorns. Yes, there were thorns strewn on the floor. I fell among them. (*She beckons to Barré*) Come here.

(BARRÉ *moves to* R *of* JEANNE *who puts her arms around his neck, pulls him down to her, whispers and then laughs*)

BARRÉ (*bleakly*) She says that she and her Sisters were compelled to form themselves into an obscene altar, and were worshipped.
JEANNE (*pulling Barré to her*) Again. (*She whispers and laughs*)
BARRÉ. She says demons tended Grandier, and her beloved Sisters incited her. You'll understand what I mean, gentlemen.

(JEANNE *again draws Barré to her. She whispers frantically, and gradually her words become audible*)

JEANNE. . . . and so we vanquished God from His house. He fled in horror at the senses fixed in men by another hand. Free of Him, we celebrated His departure again and again. To one who has known what I have known, God is dead.

(MIGNON *and* RANGIER *kneel* L *and* R *of the litter*)

JEANNE. I have found peace. (*She lies back*)

(*There is a silence.* BARRÉ, ADAM *and* MANNOURY *move down* L *and whisper together.* DE CERISAY *moves down* R. *The* LIGHTS *on the area* C *dim to* BLACK-OUT *and come up on the areas down* L *and down* R. BARRÉ *crosses to De Cerisay. While* BARRÉ *is speaking to De Cerisay,* ADAM *and* MANNOURY *move to the litter. In the dim light* ADAM *holds up the blanket and* MANNOURY *examines Jeanne*)

BARRÉ (*to De Cerisay*) This was an innocent woman.
DE CERISAY. That was no devil. She spoke with her own voice. The voice of an unhappy woman, that's all.
BARRÉ. But the degraded imagination and filthy language she has used in other depositions. These cannot spring unaided from a cloistered woman. She is a pupil.
DE CERISAY. Of Grandier?
BARRÉ. Yes.
DE CERISAY. But the man swears he's never been in the place.
BARRÉ. Not in his own person.
DE CERISAY. There must be some way of proving what she says. Will you let my people into the house? They will conduct an investigation on a police level.
BARRÉ. Proof?

(*The* CLERK *rises, moves to Barré, gives him the report of the interrogation, then exits up* R *taking his stool, table, etc., with him*)

Three of the Sisters have made statements saying that they have undergone copulation with demons and been deflowered. Mannoury has examined them, and it's true that none of them is intact.

DE CERISAY. My dear Father, I don't want to offend your susceptibilities, but we all know about the sentimental attachments which go on between the young women in these places.

(MANNOURY *and* ADAM *move down* L.

Two MONKS *enter* R *and carry* JEANNE *off* R *on the litter.* RANGIER *and* MIGNON *rise and follow them off*)

ADAM (*to Mannoury*) Well, there now.

MANNOURY. Fascinating.

ADAM. Unusual.

MANNOURY. Must say Hell can't be as dull as some people make out. Ha, ha! What?

ADAM. Such things!

MANNOURY. You know, I think a testament of this case, privately printed, might have quite a sale.

BARRÉ (*to De Cerisay*) You don't wish to be convinced.

DE CERISAY. I do. Very much. One way or another. (*He exits* R)

(ADAM *and* MANNOURY *cross to Barré*)

BARRÉ. Have you examined her?

MANNOURY. Yes. I'll let you have my report later.

BARRÉ. Can you give me anything to go on, meantime?

MANNOURY. As a professional man——

ADAM. He speaks for me.

MANNOURY. —I don't like to commit myself.

BARRÉ. Even so . . .

MANNOURY. Well, let's put it this way. There's been hanky-panky.

BARRÉ. Don't mince words. There's been fornication.

MANNOURY. Rather!

BARRÉ. Lust! She's been had.

ADAM. I'll say.

BARRÉ. Thank you, gentlemen. That's all I need.

(BARRÉ *exits down* R.

ADAM *and* MANNOURY *exit* R.

The LIGHTS *on the areas down* R *and down* L *dim to* BLACK-OUT *and come up on the area* C *for night effect.*

GRANDIER *enters* L *and moves* C. PHILLIPE *enters* R, *followed by a* SERVANT *carrying a lantern. She sees Grandier and quickly dismisses the* SERVANT *who exits* R. GRANDIER *and* PHILLIPE *meet* C)

PHILLIPE. They said you were at the Governor's house.

GRANDIER. I've just come from there. Walk to the church with me.

PHILLIPE (*moving away slightly*) No.

GRANDIER (*moving to her*) What's the matter?

PHILLIPE. I want to know. Was I restless last night? I had to leave you before it was light. I went as quietly as I could. Did I disturb you? It's important that I should know.

GRANDIER. I can't remember. Why is it important?

PHILLIPE (*moving* RC) You can't remember. (*She gives a sudden, startling harsh laugh*)

GRANDIER. Walk to the church with me.

PHILLIPE. No. There's no need to go into the confessional to say what I have to tell you. I'm pregnant.

(*There is a silence.* GRANDIER *moves down* C. *The* LIGHTS *on the area* C *increase*)

GRANDIER. So it ends.

PHILLIPE. I'm frightened.

GRANDIER. Of course. How can I own the child?

PHILLIPE. I'm very frightened.

GRANDIER. And there was such bravery in love, wasn't there, Phillipe? All through the summer nights. How unafraid we were each time we huddled down together. We laughed as we roused the animal. Remember? Now it has devoured us.

PHILLIPE. Help me.

GRANDIER. And we were to have been each other's salvation. Did I really believe it was possible?

PHILLIPE. I love you.

GRANDIER. Yes, I did believe it. I remember leaving you one day —you had been unusually adroit . . .

PHILLIPE. Oh, God!

GRANDIER. I was filled with that indecent confidence which comes after perfect coupling. And as I went I thought—yes, solemnly I thought—the body can transcend its purpose. It can become a thing of such purity that it can be worshipped to the limits of imagination. Anything is allowed. All is right. And such perfection makes for an understanding of the hideous state of existence.

PHILLIPE. Touch me.

GRANDIER. But what is it now? An egg. A thing of weariness, loathing and sickness. So it ends.

PHILLIPE. Where is love?

GRANDIER (*turning to her*) Where indeed? Go to your Father. Tell him the truth. Let him find some good man. They exist. (*He turns up* C)

PHILLIPE. Help me.

GRANDIER (*stopping and turning*) How can I help you? Take my hand.

(PHILLIPE *moves to Grandier and holds his hand*)

There. Like touching the dead, isn't it?

(PHILLIPE *releases his hand*)

Good-bye, Phillipe.

(GRANDIER *exits* R.
PHILLIPE *exits down* R.
The LIGHTS *on the area* C *dim to* BLACK-OUT *and come up on the area down* L. ADAM, MANNOURY *and* MIGNON *are in the pharmacy.*
BARRÉ *enters down* L. *He gives a harsh cry and moves like a drunken man. The others scatter in alarm*)

BARRÉ. I was denied entrance to the convent tonight. By armed guards.

MIGNON. My God, my God, what's wrong?

BARRÉ. The Archbishop has issued an ordinance against further exorcism or investigation.

MIGNON. Never!

(MANNOURY *sits on the bench*)

BARRÉ. It was done at the request of De Cerisay and D'Armagnac. What's more the Archbishop's personal physician—that rationalist fool—got hold of the women without my knowledge. He examined them, and gave it as his opinion that there was no genuine possession.

MIGNON. What shall we do? Oh, what shall we do?

BARRÉ. De Cerisay sees it as an act of justice. He doesn't understand that such things play straight into the hands of the Devil. Allow reasonable doubt for a man's sin, and the Devil snaps it up. (*He shouts wearily*) There can be no reasonable doubt in sin. All or nothing.

MIGNON. Of course. Of course. Justice has nothing to do with salvation. (*He pulls the stool forward*) Sit down. Sit down.

BARRÉ (*sitting on the stool*) My life's work is threatened by a corrupt Archbishop, a liberal doctor and an ignorant lawyer. Ah, gentlemen, there'll be happiness in hell tonight.

MANNOURY. Are we done for, then?

ADAM. Seems so.

MANNOURY. All up.

ADAM. Dear me!

MANNOURY. Pity!

MIGNON (*dropping to his knees*) Let us pray.

ADAM. I beg your pardon?

MIGNON. Let us pray.

ADAM. What for?

MIGNON. Well, let me think.

ADAM. Right you are.

MIGNON. I know.

ADAM. Yes?

MIGNON. Let us pray that the Archbishop has a diabolic vision——

BARRÉ. I shall go back to my parish.

MIGNON. —of a particularly horrible nature.

BARRÉ. There's work for me there.

MIGNON. He's an old man, too. Perhaps we can frighten him to death.

BARRÉ (*rising*) Be quiet, Mignon. You rave.

MIGNON. Don't leave us.

BARRÉ. I must.

MIGNON (*rising*) You're naturally a little depressed by this set-back. But we'll find a way.

BARRÉ. No. The Archbishop's ordinance has made evil impossible in this place. For the moment. But the ordinance doesn't apply in my parish, and you can be sure that Satan is trumpeting there. I must answer the call.

MIGNON. We shall miss you very much.

BARRÉ. My dear friend, a whisper from hell and I shall be back.

> (BARRÉ *exits down* L. ADAM, MANNOURY *and* MIGNON *exit* L.
>
> *The* LIGHTS *on the area down* L *dim to* BLACK-OUT *and come up on the area down* R. GRANDIER *enters* R, *moves* RC, *kneels and prays.* D'ARMAGNAC *and* DE CERISAY *enter* R)

D'ARMAGNAC (*as he enters*) Where's the damned priest?

GRANDIER (*rising*) I believe I must thank you, De Cerisay, for having this persecution stopped. Very well, I do so now.

DE CERISAY. I acted for you, Father, but you surely don't suppose it was entirely on your behalf. The circus up at the convent was beginning to attract a lot of unwelcome attention to the town. It's my job to keep some sort of order in the place.

D'ARMAGNAC. You don't make it easy for your friends, Grandier, Trincant has told me about his daughter. You have your whores. Why did you have to do this?

GRANDIER. It seemed a way.

D'ARMAGNAC. A way to what?

GRANDIER. I begin to understand at last that all worldly things have a single purpose for a man of my kind. Politics, power, the senses, riches, pride and authority. I choose them with the same care that you, sir, select a weapon. But my intention is different. I need to turn them against myself.

D'ARMAGNAC. To bring about your end?

GRANDIER. Yes. I have a great need to be united with God. Living has drained the need for life from me. My exercise of the senses has flagged to total exhaustion. I am a dead man, compelled to live.

D'ARMAGNAC. You disgust me. This is a sickness.

GRANDIER. No, sir. It is the meaning and purpose.

D'ARMAGNAC. I'm not one for sophisticated argument, but tell me something. I can see that the obvious short cut, self-destruction, is not possible. But isn't creating the circumstances for your death, which is what you seem to be doing, equally sinful?

GRANDIER (*moving down* R) Leave me some hope.

D'ARMAGNAC. The hope that God will smile upon your efforts to create an enemy so malignant as to bring you down, and so send you—up?

GRANDIER. Yes.

D'ARMAGNAC (*taking out a letter*) I've a letter here from Paris. It should make you happy. By supporting me in this matter of the fortifications, you have made an excellent enemy. Cardinal Richelieu. So far, the King is standing with me against the Cardinal. But should the King fail or falter, this city will come down. And you will probably have your wish, for you are deeply implicated. All the same, I shall continue to protect you from what I think to be a most dreadful course, and a most blasphemous philosophy.

GRANDIER. It is what I seek, sir. Don't hold it from me. Think what it must be like. I reach the end of a long day. I am weary, fed and satisfied. I go home. On the way, I stare at a stranger across the street, perhaps a child. I greet a friend. I lie looking down on the face of a sleeping woman. I see all these with wonder and hope, and ask myself, "Is this, perhaps, the means to my end?" And I am denied. (*He suddenly hides his face in his hands*) Oh, my God, my God! All things fail me.

D'ARMAGNAC. Afraid, Grandier?

GRANDIER. Yes. Yes. Yes. Forsaken. (*He falls to his knees down* R)

(D'ARMAGNAC *and* DE CERISAY *exit* R.

The LIGHTS *on the area down* R BLACK-OUT. GRANDIER *remains kneeling down* R. *The* LIGHTS *come up on the area* C *for bright daylight effect in the convent garden.*

GABRIELLE, CLAIRE, LOUISE *with other* NUNS *and* LAY SISTERS *enter* R *on the bridge, come down the steps and group around the area* C. GABRIELLE *takes the stool from* L *and sets it* C. JEANNE *enters* R *on the bridge, comes down the steps and sits on the stool*)

LOUISE (*to Jeanne*) What shall we do, Mother?

JEANNE. Do?

LOUISE. People are taking their children away from us.

JEANNE. Who can blame them?

CLAIRE. There's no-one to help. We have to do all the housework ourselves. It's very tiring.

JEANNE (*with sudden laughter*) Why don't you ask the devils to lend a hand?

CLAIRE. Mother!

GABRIELLE. I've taken in a little washing and sewing. I hope you don't mind, Mother.

JEANNE. Sensible girl. When hell fails to provide, one can fall back on hard work, eh?

GABRIELLE. I know you've never liked us to do menial tasks.

JEANNE. I said it diminished women in our vocation. Did I say that?

GABRIELLE. Yes.

LOUISE. Mother.

JEANNE. Yes, child?

LOUISE. Why has the Archbishop forbidden Father Barre to come and see us any more?

JEANNE. Because the Archbishop has been told that we are foolish and deluded women.

LOUISE. Mother—have we sinned?

JEANNE. By what we've done?

LOUISE. Yes. (*She kneels beside Jeanne*) Have we mocked God?

JEANNE. It was not the intention.

(*The* LIGHTS *on the area* C *dim to* BLACK-OUT.

JEANNE *and the others remain quiet and still. The sounds of a storm are heard: thunder, wind and rain. This continues during the following episode. The* LIGHTS *come up on the bridge for night effect.*

DE CERISAY *enters* R *on the bridge, carrying a lantern.* D'ARMAGNAC *enters* L *on the bridge, carrying a lantern and some pieces of paper. They meet* C. *They are wrapped against the rain and shout above the wind. They are presumed to be on the ramparts*)

DE CERISAY. D'Armagnac, are you there?

D'ARMAGNAC. The horseman fell at the gate. They found these papers scattered.

DE CERISAY. What are they?

D'ARMAGNAC. The King has gone back on his word. Richelieu has won. The town's fortifications are to come down. It is to be a little place. I shall have no more power than a tradesman. Where is the priest?

DE CERISAY (*shouting*) Grandier.

D'ARMAGNAC. He will suffer. (*He shouts*) Grandier!

(GRANDIER, *on his knees, down* R *looks up*)

GRANDIER (*rising*) What's the matter?

D'ARMAGNAC. The Cardinal has moved against us.

DE CERISAY. The King has lost his nerve.

D'ARMAGNAC. All this is to come down.

DE CERISAY. You are mentioned——

D'ARMAGNAC. We shan't stand here much longer.

DE CERISAY. —named for your resistance.

D'ARMAGNAC. You are in danger.

GRANDIER (*turning to face front*) Thank God!

D'ARMAGNAC. What do you say? I can't hear you. Are you mad? (*To De Cerisay*) Let's go down.

(D'ARMAGNAC *and* DE CERISAY *exit* R *on the bridge.
The* LIGHTS *on the bridge* BLACK-OUT. *A dim light comes up on* GRANDIER *down* R. *He kneels. The wind and rain sweep about him*)

GRANDIER. Heavenly Father, you have restored strength to my enemies, and hope to Your sinful child. I give myself into the hands of the world secure in the faith of Your mysterious ways. You have made my way possible. But You work beyond a curtain of majesty. I am afraid to raise my eyes and see. Reveal Yourself. Reveal Yourself.

(*The* LIGHTS *fade on the area down* R *and the storm noises cease.*

GRANDIER *rises and exits down* R. *The* LIGHTS *come up on the area down* L.

MIGNON, LAUBARDEMONT *and the* CAPTAIN *enter down* L)

LAUBARDEMONT. We shall have to act quickly.
MIGNON. Against Grandier? Yes. Yes.
LAUBARDEMONT. I must start for Paris tonight.
MIGNON. So soon?
LAUBARDEMONT. Can you do it in the time?
MIGNON. I can try. I wish Father Barre were here.
LAUBARDEMONT. Sort out your thoughts on the subject.
MIGNON. I've been reading it up. There was the appalling Gauffridy case. In Marseilles, twenty years ago, the priest bewitched and debauched several Ursalines . . .
LAUBARDEMONT. We don't need precedents. We need results. Here and now.

(*The* LIGHTS *come up on the area* C. MIGNON *crosses to* C. JEANNE *rises. The* NUNS *and* LAY SISTERS *group in a semicircle* LC)

MIGNON (*leading Jeanne down* C) My beloved Sisters in Christ, I am only a foolish old man who hasn't much time left on this earth to do God's Will . . .
LAUBARDEMONT (*moving up* L) Well then, get on with it.
MIGNON. My children, do you trust me?
JEANNE. Of course, Father.
MIGNON. As your spiritual instructor, do you trust me?
JEANNE. Always.
MIGNON. Very well. (*He glances at Laubardemont then sits on the stool* C) I am deeply disturbed by this sudden cessation of diabolic manifestations in you. Dreadful stories are being put about in the town and farther afield. (*He glances at Laubardemont*) They say you were not truly possessed by demons, but that you were playing parts, making a mockery both of your sublime state, and your superiors in the Church.
JEANNE. That is what we were told by the Archbishop's doctor. He talked about hysteria. The cry from the womb.
MIGNON. But as a good woman it was up to you to prove him wrong. Oh, assure me that it was true.
JEANNE. It was true.
MIGNON. You were possessed?
JEANNE. We were possessed by hell.

MIGNON (*rising*) And the instigator, the foul magician . . . ?
JEANNE. Grandier! Grandier!
NUNS. Grandier! Grandier! Grandier!

(MIGNON *glances at Laubardemont, then circles through the Nuns as he speaks*)

MIGNON. But now I fear for you in another way. The evidence is all against you. The silence of the devils condemns you. (*He pauses*) You see, they do not speak. (*He moves to Jeanne*) There is no proof of your virtue. Ah, my Sisters, this stillness presages your eternal damnation. I fear for you. I dread. Forsaken by God and forsaken by the Devil you stand in the most desolate limbo for ever. (*He kneels*) I beg you, consider your position.
JEANNE (*kneeling and clutching Mignon's hands*) Father, we are afraid.
MIGNON (*rising and crossing to* L) And well you may be, my child.
JEANNE. Don't leave us.

(*The* NUNS *kneel*)

MIGNON. What else can I do? I will pray for you. (*He turns away to Laubardemont*)

(JEANNE *grunts.* MIGNON *turns to Jeanne*)

God be praised!
LAUBARDEMONT (*to Mignon*) Well done. (*He moves down* L)

(MIGNON *moves to Jeanne. The* LIGHTS *come up on the bridge and on the area down* R)

(*To the Captain*) Get Barré back from Chinon for public exorcism at once.

(BARRÉ, RANGIER *and two* MONKS *enter* L. *One* MONK *carries a large jewelled cross and a ciborium. The other* MONK *carries Barré's robes*)

BARRÉ (*kneeling* LC) I have been sent for. A representative of the Court will attend.

(LAUBARDEMONT *and the* CAPTAIN *exit* L.
PRINCE HENRI DE CONDÉ *enters* R *on the bridge attended by two* PAGES *and two* SOLDIERS. *One of the* PAGES *carries a small relic box.* JEANNE *and the* NUNS *rise*)

LEVIATHAN (*speaking through Jeanne*) May I put in a word?
MIGNON. What is your name?
LEVIATHAN. "Leviathan."
MIGNON. Where are you lodged, unholy thing?
LEVIATHAN. In the lady's forehead.
BEHERIT (*speaking through Jeanne*) I am in the woman's stomach. My name is Beherit.

(JEANNE *grips Mignon and forces his head down to her hip*)

Isacaaron (*speaking through Jeanne*) Isacaaron speaking. From under the last rib on the left.

Elymi (*speaking through Claire*) I am here. (*With another voice*) And I.

Ehzaz (*speaking through Louise*) And I. (*With another voice*) And I am here.

(Jeanne *and the other* Nuns *become hysterical and crowd around* Mignon. *There is a clamour of diabolic voices, derisive laughter, squeals and howls.* De Condé *beckons to the* Soldiers *who move down* c, *round up the* Nuns *and herd them up* lc *where they collapse in an untidy heap, exhausted, mere rubbish on the ground.* Mignon *breaks free.* De Condé *comes down the steps, moves to Barré and regards him for a moment. The* Page *puts the relic box on the bench* r, *then the two* Pages *moves up* rc *and look at the Nuns.* Mignon *crosses to Rangier*)

De Condé. I don't wish, my dear Father, to disturb your devotions, and I would never suggest that a member of the royal family——

(Barré *rises*)

—took precedence over God—all the same . . .

Barré. I am at your service, sir.

De Condé. Thank you. These are the raving women I take it?

Barré. All of them possessed by one or more devils.

De Condé. And the instigator is a man of your own people?

Barré. A priest, yes.

De Condé. You don't seem amused.

Barré. Amused?

(*A* Servant *enters down* r *with a throne chair which he places up* rc. *He then collects a banner and stands behind the chair*)

De Condé. Never mind.

Barré. If you'll take your place, sir, I'll proceed.

De Condé. Very well. (*He sits in the throne chair*)

(Barré *moves to* Rangier *who takes the garments from the* Monk *and helps* Barré *to robe.* Mignon *takes the cross from one of the Monks*)

(*To one of the Pages*) Those are women, darling. Look well. Vomit, if you wish. No, don't touch them. Come here.

(*The* Pages *move and stand* r *and* l *of De Condé*)

Man is born of them. Gross things. Nasty. Breeding ground. Eggs hatch out in hot dung. Don't wrinkle your little nose, pet. Take this scent. (*He hands a pomander to the Page*) Some men love them. The priest Grandier, for example. He's picked the gobbets from the stew. He's . . . (*He whispers in the Page's ear*)

(*The* Page *and* De Condé *laugh.* Barré *takes the ciborium from the* Monk *and crosses to De Condé. The* Monks *kneel*)

Barré. With your permission, sir, I'll begin.
De Condé. Please do so.
Barré. But first I have a declaration to make. This, sir,—(*he holds up the ciborium*) contains the holy eucharist.

(Jeanne *snores*)

(*He faces front and holds the ciborium above his head*) Heavenly Father, I pray that I may be confounded and that the maledictions of Dathan and Abiram may fall upon me, if I have sinned or been at fault in any way in this affair.
De Condé. A very commendable gesture. Bravo!

(*The* Pages *clap.* Barré *turns towards Jeanne*)

Barré. Leviathan! Leviathan!
Leviathan (*speaking through Jeanne; sleepily*) Go away.
Barré. Rouse yourself.
Leviathan. You bore me.
Barré. I am only a humble man but I speak in the name of our Lord Jesus Christ.

(Jeanne *looks through a Soldier's legs*)

Leviathan (*speaking through Jeanne*) Don't keep bringing that impostor's name into the conversation.
Barré. It disturbs you, eh?
De Condé. Reverend Father, I notice that you don't speak to these creatures in Latin, as is usual. Why is that?
Barré. They're not conversant with the language. You'll understand, sir, that there are uneducated as well as educated devils.
De Condé. Quite.

(Jeanne *looks through the Soldier's legs*)

Leviathan (*speaking through Jeanne*) I haven't travelled much.

(*There is deep laughter, taken up by the other Devils*)

Barré. Listen, filth . . .
Leviathan. You're always so personal.
Barré. I'm going to speak a name to you. Grandier.
Leviathan. Oh, that's a sweet noise. Do it again.

(Jeanne *and the* Nuns *rise*)

Barré. Grandier.
Leviathan. Yes, I like that.
Barré. You know him?
Leviathan. We serve him. Don't we?
Devils (*speaking through the Nuns*) Grandier! Grandier!

(*There is pandemonium. The* Nuns *put their arms round the Soldiers' necks. The* Soldiers *push the Nuns to the floor.* Mignon *steps forward with the cross held high over the Nuns. The* Pages *laugh and clap. The screams and shouts gradually die away.* Jeanne *collapses on the ground down* c)

De Condé. Father, may I question these things?
Barré. By all means, sir.

(*The general* Lighting *comes up to full.* De Condé *rises, moves* c *and stands above Jeanne*)

De Condé (*addressing the Nuns*) Gentlemen, you have given us your view on the character and work of our Blessed Saviour.

(*There is hissing from the* Devils)

Quite so. Which of you will answer me on a matter of merely national importance?
Beherit (*speaking through Jeanne*) I'll try.
De Condé. You will? Good. What's your name?
Beherit. "Beherit."
De Condé. Well, Beherit, tell me this. What's your opinion of His Majesty, the King of France and his adviser, the great Cardinal? (*He pauses*)

(Jeanne *turns and faces front*)

De Condé. Come now, as a political devil you must have some views. Or do you find yourself in the quandary of most Oppositions? Having to speak with more than one voice.
Beherit (*muttering*) Don't understand.
De Condé. You understand very well. If you, Beherit, devil, praise the King and his Minister, you imply that their policy is hellish. If you, Reverend Mother, a woman, dispraise them, you run the risk of treason against powerful men. I sympathize with your difficulty. (*He beckons to a Page*)

(*The* Page *picks up the relic box from the bench* r *and hands it to* De Condé)

Father, I have here a relic of most holy worth. It has been lent to me by a great cathedral of the North. I feel the bits and pieces which you've assembled from local sources may not be powerful enough to dispel these impudent demons. So why not try this?
Barré. What is in the box, sir?
De Condé. A phial of the blood of our Lord Jesus Christ.

(De Condé *takes the box in turn to* Rangier *and* Mignon *who kneel and kiss it. He then takes the box to* Barré *who reverently takes it in his hands and kisses it*)

Tell me, Father, what effect would the close proximity of this relic have on devils such as these?
Barré. It would put them to flight.

DE CONDÉ. At once?

BARRÉ. Immediately. I couldn't guarantee, of course, that when the relic was removed, they wouldn't return.

DE CONDÉ. Of course not. That would be asking too much. Would you like to try?

(BARRÉ *moves* C)

BARRÉ. In the name of our Heavenly Father, I conjure thee, most frightful beings, by this most sacred substance, to depart. (*He applies the box on Jeanne's forehead*)

(JEANNE *throws herself back and screams. The* NUNS *scream. At once, in a number of horrible screams, the* DEVILS *leave their bodies by way of their distorted mouths. There is a silence.* BARRÉ *holds the box up triumphantly then* JEANNE *rises to her full height. She speaks calmly, with the voice of a young girl, in her own person. The* NUNS *all stand*)

JEANNE (*quietly*) I am free! I am free! (*She goes to De Condé, kneels and kisses his hands*)

DE CONDÉ (*whipping his hands away from Jeanne*) I'm very pleased to have been of some service, madam. (*He crosses to Barré*)

BARRÉ (*triumphantly*) You see!

(DE CONDÉ *takes the box from Barré, opens it, holds it upside down and displays it around. It is empty*)

DE CONDÉ. You see, Father?

BARRÉ (*after a moment*) Ah, sir, what sort of trick have you played on us?

DE CONDÉ. Reverend sir, what sort of trick are you playing on us?

(DE CONDÉ *and the* PAGES *move down* R. *There is silence for a few moments,* DE CONDÉ *smiling, the hushed crowd of* WOMEN, *terrified—the silence is broken by* MIGNON. *He starts to run in circles, and demoniac laughter is heard. The* NUNS *are possessed. They scream and rock hysterically—*MIGNON *seizes* CLAIRE *and dances with her*)

LEVIATHAN (*speaking through Mignon*) Fooled again!

BEHERIT (*speaking through Mignon*) Make way.

(RANGIER *joins in the melee, possessed. Only* JEANNE *stands alone and still. One of the* PAGES *laughs in a ringing, hysterical manner.* BARRÉ *stares about him in horror, then wielding the cross like a club, he plunges among the crowd, laying about him*)

BARRÉ. We are besieged. Clear the place at once.

(*The* SOLDIERS *herd the* NUNS *off* L.
MIGNON *dances off* R *with* CLAIRE.
RANGIER *follows them off, doing handstands*)

BARRÉ (*he passes among the crowd, laying the cross on possessed and unpossessed alike, and shouting) Per factorem mundi, per eum qui habet potestatem mittendi te in gehennam, ut ab hoc famulo Dei, qui ad sinum Ecclesiae recarrit, cum metu et exercitu furoris tui festinus discedas.*

(ALL except *Jeanne, De Condé and the two Pages have gone.*
BARRÉ *follows the last of them off.*
The LIGHTS *dim to* BLACK-OUT *except for the areas down* R *and down* L. JEANNE *moves down* L. *A* SERVANT *removes the throne chair. A* PAGE *still laughs)*

DE CONDÉ (*smiling*) Be quiet, child.

(*The* PAGE *is silent*)

(*He stares across at Jeanne*) Mother, I am often accused of being a libertine. Very well. Being born so high I have to stoop lower than other men. Soiled, dabbling myself, I know what I am doing and what I must give. But do you know what you must give to have your wish about this man Grandier? I will tell you. Your immortal soul to damnation in an infinite desert of eternal bestiality. (*To the Pages*) Come, darlings.

(DE CONDÉ *exits* L *on the bridge.*
The PAGES *follow him off.*
The LIGHTS *come up on the area* C.
LOUISE *and* CLAIRE *enter gaily* R. LOUISE *has a hand mirror.* JEANNE *remains down* L)

CLAIRE (*as she enters; in a gay voice*) Give it to me.

(LOUISE *looks at herself in the mirror*)

I was never any good at prayer.
LOUISE. Neither was I.
CLAIRE. We could have spent our lives on our knees.
LOUISE. And no-one would have heard of us.
CLAIRE. They're selling my picture in the town.
LOUISE. We're famous all over France.
CLAIRE. Are you still worried about being damned?
LOUISE. Not any more.
CLAIRE. Not since your beautiful legs have been so admired.
LOUISE (*turning to Claire*) Sweetheart, what do you think of in chapel, now?
CLAIRE. This and that. New ways.
LOUISE. To amuse?
CLAIRE. Yes.

(NUNS *are heard in the distance, singing Plainsong*)

(*She grabs the mirror*) Come on.

(CLAIRE, *laughing, exits* R. LOUISE *follows her off.*
The LIGHTS *on the area* C *and down* R BLACK-OUT. JEANNE *stands silent for a moment*)

LEVIATHAN (*speaking through Jeanne*) Clear your mind of cant, you absurd little monster.

JEANNE. I'm afraid.

LEVIATHAN. Nonsense! We'll support you in anything you want to do.

JEANNE. I wish to be pure.

LEVIATHAN. There is no such thing.

JEANNE. Oh, God—God, yes, there is.

LEVIATHAN. No, there isn't. Now think, my dear. Remember the night-time visions. He came and . . . (*He giggles obscenely*) Oh, that thing . . . and you, agape—no, no, my darling, not purity, not even dignity.

(*The singing ceases*)

LEVIATHAN. What are you thinking of? Not only all impure, not all absurd. Remember?

(JEANNE *starts to laugh.* LEVIATHAN *joins in. The* LIGHTS *down* L *dim to* BLACK-OUT.

JEANNE *exits* L *in the* BLACK-OUT.

A trumpet sounds in the distance. The LIGHTS *come up on the bridge, on the area* C *and on the area down* R *for night effect.*

LOUIS *and* RICHELIEU *enter* R *on the bridge and move to* C *of it. It is a Council of State.*

LAUBARDEMONT *and the* CAPTAIN *enter down* R *and move* C *and bow*)

LAUBARDEMONT. Your Majesty. Your Eminence. You have asked me to report on the case of possession at Loudun.

(DE CONDÉ *enters down* R, *crosses to* C *and bows*)

The man's name is Urbain Grandier.

DE CONDÉ. He is innocent. (*He bows and moves* R)

LAUBARDEMONT. I have been advised by priests of the diocese and by reputable medical men that the possession is genuine.

DE CONDÉ. I have also been there. The possession is false.

LAUBARDEMONT. Grandier's house has been searched. Various manuscripts have been found. There was a pamphlet written some years ago and directed against Your Eminence. Other papers confirm Grandier's support of D'Armagnac in his defiant attitude about the fortifications of the town, which has distressed you so much, Your Majesty. There were letters and notebooks of a more personal kind. A treatise on Sacerdotal Celibacy was found. The man seems to have been in love when this was written. It is reported that a mock marriage took place with a daughter of the Public Prosecutor. There were letters from other women, one of which appears to suggest that he has committed the veneric act in church.

DE CONDÉ. (*Moving* C) For the love of Jesus Christ, if you wish to destroy the man, then destroy him. I'm not here to plead for his life. But your methods are shameful. He deserves better. Any man does. Kill him with power, but don't pilfer his house, and hold evidence of this sort against him. What man could face arraignment on the idiocy of youth, old love letters, and the pathetic objects stuffed in drawers or at the bottom of cupboards, kept for the fear that one day he would need to be reminded that he was once loved? No. (*He moves* R) Destroy a man for his opposition, his strength, or his Majesty. But not for this.

(*There is a silence*)

(*To the Council*) I should now give you any evidence in the man's favour.

RICHELIEU (*moving down the steps to Laubardemont*) The Devil must never be believed, even when he tells the truth.

LAUBARDEMONT. I shall act on your instructions at once.

(*He kisses Richelieu's hand and exits* L.
The CAPTAIN *follows him off.* RICHELIEU *exits* R *on the bridge.*
LOUIS *and* DE CONDÉ *exit* L *on the bridge.*
The LIGHTS *on the bridge dim to* BLACK-OUT. *The church bells are heard.* GRANDIER *enters* L. *He carries a box and a bunch of flowers.*
The SEWERMAN *enters down* R *carrying his bucket and spade. He meets Grandier down* C *and puts down his bucket and spade*)

SEWERMAN (*looking at the flowers*) Why, whatever's this?

GRANDIER. I must have picked them somewhere. I can't remember. You have them.

SEWERMAN (*taking the flowers*) Thank you. (*He puts the flowers on the bucket, then sits on the ground*) They smell sweet. Very suitable.

GRANDIER. Can I sit with you?

SEWERMAN. Of course.

(GRANDIER *puts down his box and sits on it*)

I've no sins this morning, though. Sorry.

GRANDIER. Let me look at you.

(*The* LIGHTS *on the area down* R *dim to* BLACK-OUT)

SEWERMAN. Do you like what you see?

GRANDIER. Very much.

SEWERMAN. What's happened?

GRANDIER. I've been out of town. An old man was dying. I sat with him for two nights and a day. I was seeing death for the hundredth time. It was an obscene struggle. It always is. Once again a senile, foolish and sinful old man had left it rather late to come to terms. He held my hand so tightly that I could not move. His grimy face stared up at me in blank surprise at what was happening to him. He was dirty and old and not very bright. And I loved him so much. I envied him so much, for he was standing on the threshold of everlasting life. I wanted him to turn his face to God. I said to him, "Be glad, be glad." But he did not understand. His spirit weakened at dawn. It could not mount another day. I took out the necessary properties which I travel in this box. The vulgar little sins were confessed, absolved, and the man could die. He did so. Brutally, holding on to the last. I spoke my usual words to the family, with my priest's face. My duty was done. But I could not forget my love for the man. I came out of the house. I thought I'd walk back, air myself after the death cell. I was very tired. The road was dusty. I remembered the day I came here. I was wearing new shoes. They were white with dust. Do you know, I flicked them over with my stole before being received by the Bishop. I was vain and foolish, then. Ambitious, too. I walked on. I could see my church in the distance. I thought of my love for the beauty of this not very beautiful place. And I remembered night in the building, with the gold, lit by candlelight, against the darkness. I thought of you. I remembered you as a friend. I rested. The country was stretched out. Do you know where the rivers join? I once made love there. Yes, I was very tired. I could see far beyond the point my eyes could see. Castles, cities, mountains, oceans, plains, forests, and . . . And then —oh, my son, my son—and then—I want to tell you . . . (*He breaks off*)

SEWERMAN. Do so. Be calm.

GRANDIER. My son, I . . . Am I mad?

SEWERMAN. No. Go on. Tell me. What did you do?

GRANDIER. I created God. (*He pauses*) I created Him from the light and the air, from the dust of the road, from the sweat of my hands, from gold, from filth, from the memory of women's faces, from great rivers, from children. I caused Him to be from fear and despair. I gathered in everything for this mighty act, all I have known, seen and experienced. My sin, my presumption, my vanity, my love, my hate, my lust. And last I gave myself and so made God. And he was magnificent. For He is all these things. I was utterly in His presence. I knelt by the road. I took out the bread and the wine. *Panem vinum in salutis consecramas hostian.* And in this understanding He gave Himself humbly and faithfully to me, as I had given myself to Him.

(*There is a silence*)

SEWERMAN. You've found peace.

GRANDIER. More. I've found meaning. I must go now. (*He rises*) I must go to worship Him in His house, adore Him in His shrine. I must go to church. (*He picks up his box*)

(GRANDIER *exits* R.

The SEWERMAN *rises, picks up the bucket and flowers and exits* L. *The* LIGHTS *dim to* BLACK-OUT. *The stained glass window is lowered from the flies. The* LIGHTS *come up on the area* C.

LAUBARDEMONT *enters* R *and crosses to* C. *The* CAPTAIN *follows him on.* GRANDIER *enters*)

LAUBARDEMONT (*intercepting Grandier* RC) You are forbidden this place.

GRANDIER. Forbidden?

LAUBARDEMONT. You are an impious and libertine priest. You must not enter.

GRANDIER. It is my church. My beloved church!

LAUBARDEMONT. No longer. You're under arrest. Charges will be read. Come with me. (*To the Captain*) Bring him.

LAUBARDEMONT *exits* R.

The LIGHTS *dim to* BLACK-OUT *as*

the CURTAIN *falls*

ACT III

When the CURTAIN *rises, the stage is in darkness, then the* LIGHTS *come up on the area* C. *An iron grille with a gate in it is set* C. GRANDIER *is sitting on a bale of straw down stage of the grille, in the cell.* BONTEMPS, *the gaoler, enters behind the grille, carrying a bucket of water and a ladle.*

BONTEMPS (*outside the gate*) Have you slept? (*He unlocks the gate*)

GRANDIER. No. No, the noise. The crowd. Have they slept?

BONTEMPS (*coming into the cell and closing the gate*) Thirty thousand have come into the town. (*He puts down the bucket*) Where do you expect them to find beds?

GRANDIER. Why should they want to sleep, anyway? Did I, as a child, the night before a treat?

BONTEMPS. They're certainly looking forward to it.

GRANDIER. What? Say it.

BONTEMPS. The execution.

GRANDIER. I haven't been tried yet.

BONTEMPS. All right. Have it your own way. The trial, then. (*He hands Grandier a ladle full of water*)

GRANDIER. Are you a merciful man? (*He drinks*)

BONTEMPS. Look, this is your system. Just be thankful that you can get men to do the job. Don't ask that they should be humans as well. I came to tell you that you're to be called early. So try and get some sleep.

GRANDIER (*returning the ladle to Bontemps*) Thank you.

BONTEMPS. Is there anything you want? There's not much I can offer.

GRANDIER. Nothing. Nothing.

(BONTEMPS *picks up the bucket, goes out of the cell, locks the door and exits* R.

The LIGHTS *on the area* C *dim to* BLACK-OUT *and come up on the area down* R.

JEANNE *and* MIGNON *enter down* R. GRANDIER *remains in the cell*)

MIGNON. I must go now.

JEANNE. No.

MIGNON. It's three o'clock in the morning. I'm an old man, need some sleep.

JEANNE. I don't want to be left alone with him.

MIGNON. With your persecutor? Grandier?

JEANNE. Yes.

MIGNON. He's under close guard.

JEANNE. No. He's here. Within me. Like a child. He never

revealed to me what sort of man he was. I knew him to be beautiful. Many said he was clever and many said he was wicked. But for all his violence to my soul and body he never came to me in anything but love.

MIGNON. My Sister . . .

JEANNE. No, let me speak. He's within me, I say. I'm—possessed. But he is still, lying beneath my heart. Living through my breath and my blood. And he makes me afraid. Afraid that I may have fallen in the gravest error in this matter.

MIGNON. What do you mean?

JEANNE. Have I been mistaken? Did Satan take on the person of my love, my darling, so as to delude me?

MIGNON. Never. The man is his agent.

JEANNE (*turning away from Mignon*) I have such a little body. It is a small battleground in which to decide this terrible struggle between good and evil, between love and hate. Was I wrong to allow it?

MIGNON. No, no. Don't you understand? These very thoughts are put in your mind by the Devil. It's wrong to believe that hell always fights with the clamour of arms. It is now, in the small hours, that Satan sends his secret agents, whispering with their messages of doubt.

JEANNE (*kneeling*) I don't know. I don't know. You all speak with so many voices. And I am very tired.

(MIGNON *blesses Jeanne and exits* R)

(*She cries out*) Father! Father!

(JEANNE *rises and exits* R.
The LIGHTS *on the area down* R BLACK-OUT *and come up on the area* RC. GRANDIER *is seated alone in the cell*)

GRANDIER. There will be pain. It will kill God. My fear is driving Him out already. That morning on the road. What was that? It was a little delusion of meaning. A trick of the sun, some fatigue of the body, and a man starts to believe that he's immortal. Look at me now. Wringing my hands, trying to convince myself that this flesh and bone is meaningful. Sad, sad, though, very sad. To make a man see in the morning what the glory might be, and by night to snatch it from him. This need to create a meaning. What arrogance it is. Expendable, that's what we are. Nothing proceeding to nothing. (*He drops to his knees*) Most Heavenly Father, though I struggle in Your arms like a fretful child . . . No. No. We are flies upon the wall. Buzzing in the heat. That's so. That's so. No, no, we're monsters made up in a day. Clay in a baby's hands. Horrible. We should be bottled and hung in the pharmacy. Curiosities, for amusement only. Most Heavenly Father, let me look into this void. Let me look into myself. Is there one thing, past or present, which makes for a purpose? (*He pauses*) Nothing. Nothing.

(Bontemps *and* Father Ambrose, *an old man, enter behind the grille.* Ambrose *carries some books*)

(*He rises and turns*) Who's there?

Ambrose. My name is Ambrose.

(Bontemps *unlocks and opens the gate*)

Grandier. I know you, Father.

Ambrose (*coming into the cell*) I was told of your trouble, my son. The night can be very long.

Grandier. Yes.

Ambrose. I thought I might read to you. Or, if you'd like it better, we can pray together.

Grandier. No.

(Ambrose *turns to go*)

Stay with me.

(Ambrose *stops and turns.* Bontemps *closes the gate, locks it and exits* R)

Help me.

Ambrose. I will try.

Grandier (*sitting on the bale*) They are destroying my faith. By fear and loneliness, now. Later, by pain.

Ambrose. Go to God, my son.

Grandier. Nothing going to nothing.

Ambrose. God is here, and Christ is now.

Grandier. Yes. That is my faith. But how can I defend it?

Ambrose. By remembering the will of God.

Grandier. Yes. Yes.

Ambrose. By remembering that nothing must be asked of Him, and nothing refused.

Grandier (*rising*) Yes. But this is all in the books. I've read them and understood them. And it is not enough. Not enough. Not now.

Ambrose. God is here, and Christ is here.

Grandier. You're an old man. (*He moves to the grille*) Have you gathered no more than this fustian in all your years?

(Ambrose *moves to the gate*)

Wait. I'm sorry. You came in pure charity. The only one who has done so. I'm sorry.

(Ambrose *moves to the bale and sits*)

Ambrose. Suffering must be willed, affliction must be willed, humiliation must be willed, and in the act of willing . . .

Grandier. They'll be understood. I know. I know.

Ambrose. Then you know everything.

Grandier. I know nothing. Speak to me as a man, Father. Talk about simple things.

Ambrose. I came to help you, my son.

Grandier. You can help me. By speaking as a man. So shut your books.

(Ambrose *puts his books down beside him*)

Forget other men's words. Speak to me.

Ambrose. Ah, you believe there is some secret in simplicity. I am a simple man, it's true. I've never had any great doubt. Plain and shy, I have been less tempted than others, of course. The Devil likes more magnificence than I've ever been able to offer. A peasant boy who clung to the love of God because he was too awkward to ask for the love of man. I'm not a good example, my son. That's why I brought the books.

Grandier. You think too little of yourself. What must we give God?

Ambrose. Ourselves.

Grandier. But I am unworthy.

Ambrose. Have you greatly sinned?

Grandier. Greatly.

Ambrose. Even young girls come to me nowadays and confess things I don't know about. So it's hardly likely that I'll understand the sins of a young man of the world such as yourself. But let me try.

Grandier. There have been women and lust; power and ambition, worldliness and mockery.

Ambrose. Remember. God is here. You speak before Him. Christ is now. You suffer with Him.

Grandier (*moving down* c) I dread the pain to come. The humiliation.

Ambrose. Did you dread the ecstasy of love?

Grandier. No.

Ambrose. Or its humiliation?

Grandier. I gloried in it. I have lived by the senses.

Ambrose. Then die by them.

Grandier. What did you say?

Ambrose. Offer God pain, convulsion and disgust.

Grandier. Yes. Yes.

Ambrose. Let Him reveal Himself in the only way you can understand.

Grandier. Yes. Give Him myself.

Ambrose. It is all any of us can do. We live a little while, and in that little while we sin. We go to Him as we can. All is forgiven.

Grandier. Yes, I am His child. It is true. Let Him take me as I am. So there is meaning, after all. It is not nothing going to nothing. It is sin going to forgiveness. It is a human creature going to love.

(Bontemps *enters* r, *unlocks and opens the gate*)

BONTEMPS. He's got to leave. If you want a priest they say you can ask for Father Barre or Father Rangier. He's got to leave. They said so. Out there.

AMBROSE (*rising*) Must I go?

GRANDIER. Yes, Father. You are dangerous in your innocence. But they are too late.

AMBROSE. I don't understand.

GRANDIER (*picking up the books and giving them to Ambrose*) It is better that way. Father, let me kiss you. (*He kisses Ambrose*)

(AMBROSE *goes out of the cell and exits* R.
BONTEMPS *closes the gate, locks it and exits* R)

What? Tears? When was the last time this happened? What are they for? They must be for what is lost, not for what has been found. For God is here.

(*The* LIGHTS *on the area* C *are dimmed and come up on the area down* R.
GABRIELLE *and* LOUISE *enter down* R, *laughing*)

GABRIELLE. The town's like a fairground.

(CLAIRE *runs on* R)

CLAIRE. They were singing not far from my window all night.

GABRIELLE. There are acrobats. I wish we could see them. I love acrobats.

CLAIRE. Haven't we entertained each other enough in that way?

(GABRIELLE, LOUISE *and* CLAIRE *exit* R, *laughing*.
The LIGHTS *fade on the area down* R *and come up on the area* C.
BONTEMPS *enters* R, *unlocks the cell gate and opens it*)

BONTEMPS. Come on.

(BONTEMPS *and* GRANDIER *exit* R.
There is a pause.
MANNOURY *enters* R *and comes into the cell.* ADAM *enters* L, *sees* MANNOURY *and speaks to him through the grille. He carries a bag*)

ADAM. Hullo.

MANNOURY. Hullo.

ADAM. Were you sent for?

MANNOURY. Yes.

ADAM. So was I. By De Laubardemont.

MANNOURY. That's it.

ADAM (*coming into the cell*) I've brought my things. Have you?

MANNOURY. Yes.

ADAM. What I thought would be necessary.

MANNOURY. Difficult to say, isn't it?

ADAM. Have you done this before?

MANNOURY. No.

ADAM. Neither have I. Hm! Cold in here.

MANNOURY. Yes.
ADAM. Cold out.
MANNOURY. 'Tis.
ADAM. For a summer day.
MANNOURY. August. Yes.

(LAUBARDEMONT *and* BONTEMPS *enter* R. LAUBARDEMONT *come;
into the cell.* BONTEMPS *remains outside by the gate*)

LAUBARDEMONT. Good morning, gentlemen. Glad to find you
here. He's being brought back from the court. Should be on his way
now.
MANNOURY. What exactly do you want us to do?
LAUBARDEMONT. Prepare the man. A decision has been reached.
Unanimously. He is condemned.
ADAM. Well, well!
MANNOURY. Not surprising.
ADAM. There it is.
LAUBARDEMONT. I want you to be as quick as you can. There was
an extraordinary amount of sympathy for the creature when he
made his statement. There were even some unhealthy tears. So I
want him ready and back to the court to hear the sentence as soon
as possible.
MANNOURY. We'll do our best.
LAUBARDEMONT. Adam, would you be good enough to go and see
the gaoler? He's getting all the necessary stuff together. Bring it in
when he's done.
ADAM. All right.

(ADAM *goes out of the cell. He and* BONTEMPS *exit* R)

LAUBARDEMONT. The man made something of an impression.
Father Barre explained that it was the Devil's doing. He said the
calm was the brazen insolence of hell, and the dignity nothing but
unrepentant pride. Still the man made quite an impression.

(GRANDIER *enters* R *escorted by the* CAPTAIN *and two* SOLDIERS.
GRANDIER *is dressed in full canonicals, looking his finest. They come into
the cell*)

GRANDIER. Good morning, Mr Surgeon.
MANNOURY. And good morning to you.
GRANDIER. De Laubardemont I've already seen.
LAUBARDEMONT. You must return to the court at once.
GRANDIER. Very well.
LAUBARDEMONT. For the sentence.
GRANDIER. I understand.
LAUBARDEMONT. So now I must ask you to undress.
GRANDIER. Undress?
LAUBARDEMONT. You can't go like that.

GRANDIER. I suppose not.

(ADAM *enters* R *and comes into the cell. He carries a razor and strop.*

BONTEMPS *follows* ADAM *on, carrying a tray on which there is a bowl of water, an empty silver cup, a bottle of oil and a small towel. Concealed under the towel are make-up materials, bald eyebrows, spirit gum, mirror and bald pate*)

Good morning, Mr Chemist. What have you got there?

(BONTEMPS *puts the tray on the table*)

ADAM (*stammering*) It's a razor.

GRANDIER (*after a pause, to Laubardemont*) Must it be this way?

LAUBARDEMONT. Yes. Order of the Court. (*He moves up* L *in the cell*)

(ADAM *hooks the strop on to the grille and strops the razor*)

GRANDIER. Well, Mr Surgeon, all your study and training have brought you only to this. Those late nights spent discussing the existence of existence have brought you only here. To be a barber.

LAUBARDEMONT. Get on with it.

GRANDIER. Just a moment. (*He touches his black curls and then fingers his moustaches*) Have you a glass?

LAUBARDEMONT. No, no. Of course not.

BONTEMPS. There's this. (*He takes an empty silver cup from the tray, polishes the base of the cup on his sleeve and hands it to Mannoury*)

(MANNOURY *hands the cup to* GRANDIER *who looks long and deeply at his reflection. He returns the cup to Mannoury and kneels beside the tray. The* CAPTAIN, MANNOURY, ADAM, BONTEMPS *and the* SOLDIERS *surround* GRANDIER, *masking him as he unrobes. The* LIGHTS *on the area* C *dim to* BLACK-OUT *and come up on the areas down* R *and down* L. *The murmuring of a large crowd is heard.*

BARRÉ, RANGIER *and* MIGNON *enter and stand down* R. D'ARMAGNAC *and* DE CERISAY *enter and stand down* L. LAUBARDEMONT *moves down* LC. *A* CLERK *enters down* L *carrying a parchment and a gavel. He raps with the gavel on the bench down* L. *There is a sudden silence. All heads turn towards the* CLERK)

CLERK (*reading*) "Urbain Grandier, you have been found guilty of commerce with the Devil. And that you used this unholy alliance to possess, seduce and debauch certain Sisters of the holy order of St Ursula. They are fully named in this document. You also have been found guilty of obscenity, blasphemy and sacrilege. It is ordered that you proceed and kneel at the doors of St Peter's and St Ursula's and there, with a rope round your neck and a two pound taper in your hand, ask pardon of God, the King and Justice. Next, it is ordered that you be taken to the Place Sainte-Croix, tied to a stake and burned alive; after which your ashes will be scattered to the four winds. It has been decided that a commemorative plaque shall be set up in the Ursalines' chapel. The cost of this, yet to be ascertained, will be chargeable to your confiscated estate. Lastly, before sentence is carried out, you will be subjected to the Question, both ordinary and extraordinary. Pronounced at Loudun, the eighteenth of August, sixteen-thirty-four, and executed the same day."

(*The* LIGHTS *come up on the area* c. *The group around* GRANDIER *splits up. The* SOLDIERS *push* GRANDIER *down* c, *then exit* R, *taking Grandier's robes with them.* GRANDIER *is completely shaven. Gone are the magnificent curls, the moustaches, even the eyebrows. He wears only a long vivid yellow gown, impregnated with sulphur, and slippers. He stands, a bald fool.*

BONTEMPS *collects the bale, the tray, etc., and exits with them* R. *Re-enters and stands at the cell gate.* ADAM *and* MANNOURY *move* L. *As* GRANDIER *is pushed down* c *loud gasps of horror from the crowd are heard*)

(*He raps with his gavel*) Silence!

GRANDIER. My Lords, I am innocent. I am innocent, and I am afraid. I fear for my salvation. I am prepared to go and meet God, but the horrible torment you have ordered for me on the way may drive my wretched soul to despair. Despair, my Lords. It is the gravest of sins. It is the short way to eternal damnation. Surely in your wisdom you do not mean to kill a soul. So may I ask you, in your mercy to mitigate, if only a little, my punishment. (*He looks from face to face*)

(*There is a silence*)

Very well. When I was a child I was told about the martyrs. I loved the men and women who died for the honour of Jesus Christ. In a time of loneliness I have often wished to be of their company. Now, foolish and obscure priest that I am, I cannot presume to place myself among these great and holy men. But may I say that I have the hope in my heart that as this day ends, Almighty God, my beloved Father in Heaven, will glance aside and let my suffering atone for my vain and disordered life. Amen.

(*The crowd are heard to murmur "Amen"*)

LAUBARDEMONT (*to the Clerk*) Clear the court. (*He turns to Grandier*) Confess your guilt. Tell us the names of your accomplices. Then perhaps, my Lords, the judges will consider your appeal.

GRANDIER. I cannot name accomplices I've never had, nor confess to crimes I've not done.

LAUBARDEMONT. This attitude will do you no good. You will suffer for it.

GRANDIER. I know that. And I am proud.

LAUBARDEMONT. Proud, sir? That word does not become your situation. Now, look here, my dear fellow—(*he takes out a document and quill*) this document is a simple confession. Here is a pen. Just put your name to this paper and we can forget the next stage of the proceedings.

GRANDIER. You must excuse me. No. My conscience forbids me to put my name to something which is untrue.

LAUBARDEMONT. You'll save us all a lot of trouble if you'll sign. The document being true, of course. (*He shouts*) True! You've been found guilty.

GRANDIER. I'm sorry.

LAUBARDEMONT. I fear for you, Grandier. I fear for you very much. I have seen men before you take this brave standing in the chance of the Question. It was unwise, Grandier. Think again.

GRANDIER. No.

LAUBARDEMONT. You will go into the darkness before your death. Let me talk to you for a moment about pain. It is very difficult for us standing here, both healthy men, to imagine the shattering effect of agony. The sun's warm on your face at the moment, isn't it? And you can curl your toes if you want in your slippers. You are alive, and you know it. But when you are stretched out in that little room, with the pain screaming through you like a voice, let me tell you what you will think. First, "How can man do this to man?" Then, "How can God allow it?" Then, "There can be no God." Then, "There is no God."

(BARRÉ, RANGIER *and* MIGNON *cross themselves*)

The voice of pain will grow stronger, and your resolution weaker. Despair, Grandier. You used the word yourself. You called it the gravest sin. Don't reject God at this moment. Reconcile yourself. For you have bitterly offended Him. Confess.

GRANDIER. No.

(*There is a pause.* LAUBARDEMONT *paces to* LC *then back to Grandier*)

LAUBARDEMONT. Very well. I ask you once more. Once more. Will you sign?

(GRANDIER *shakes his head*)

Take him away. (*He moves up* LC)

(BONTEMPS *moves to Grandier*)

GRANDIER. I would like to ask something.

LAUBARDEMONT (*turning*) What?

GRANDIER. May I have Father Ambrose with me?

LAUBARDEMONT. No.

GRANDIER. He's a harmless old man. He won't impede you.

LAUBARDEMONT. He's no longer in the town. He's been sent away. If you want spiritual consolation, address yourself to one of these gentlemen.

(LAUBARDEMONT *exits* R.

ADAM, MANNOURY *and the* CLERK *exit up* R.

BONTEMPS *moves to Grandier.* GRANDIER *stares at Barré, Rangier and Mignon for a moment, then turns away and* BONTEMPS *leads him into the cell.*

BONTEMPS *closes and locks the cell gate then exits* R.

The LIGHTS *on the area* C *dim to* BLACK-OUT. DE CERISAY *and* D'ARMAGNAC *are down* L. *Their words will not be heard by Barré, Rangier and Mignon who are down* R)

DE CERISAY. Laubardemont's a bigger fool than I thought.

D'ARMAGNAC. Does he believe what he's saying?

DE CERISAY. Yes. Touching, isn't it?

MIGNON (*to Rangier*) I found the Commissioner's last appeal very moving.

RANGIER. Very.

BARRÉ. I suppose you understand that Grandier's refusal to sign was the final proof of guilt.

MIGNON. Yes. Yes, I suppose so.

BARRÉ. Lucifer has sealed his mouth; hardened his heart against repentance.

MIGNON. Of course. That's the reason.

BARRÉ. Shall we go?

(BARRÉ, RANGIER *and* MIGNON *exit down* R)

D'ARMAGNAC. Come to my house with me, De Cerisay.

DE CERISAY. All right, sir.

D'ARMAGNAC. I don't want you to talk to me.

DE CERISAY. Very well.

D'ARMAGNAC. We'll just sit together. And think over the day. Two—I hope—reasonable men. We'll sit and—we'll drink. Yes, that's it, we'll get drunk. Drunk enough to see visions. Come on.

(D'ARMAGNAC *and* DE CERISAY *exit down* L.

The LIGHTS *come up down* C *leaving the cell in shadow. It is a hot day in the convent garden.*

JEANNE *enters down* R *and moves down* C. *She is bare-headed and dressed only in a white, simple undergarment. Her little, deformed person looks childlike. She has a rope around her neck and carries a candle in her hand.*

CLAIRE, GABRIELLE *and* LOUISE *enter down* L *and stand frightened, watching Jeanne.* LOUISE *carries a cloak. After a few moments* CLAIRE *moves to* L *of Jeanne)*

CLAIRE. Come in, dear Mother.

JEANNE. No, child.

CLAIRE. But the sun is very hot after the rain. It will do you no good.

JEANNE. Find me a place—it needn't be so high—where I can tie this rope.

CLAIRE. No, Mother. It is the most terrible sin.

JEANNE. Sin?

CLAIRE. Yes. (*She takes the rope from Jeanne*)

LOUISE (*moving to Jeanne*) Don't frighten us, Mother. (*She puts the cloak around Jeanne and takes the candle from her*)

JEANNE. I have been woken night after night by the sound of terrible weeping. I've gone about trying to find out who it is. I have a heart, like anyone else. It can be broken by such a sound.

CLAIRE. It is the devil. He can snivel to order.

GABRIELLE. Yes, Mother, think. Father Grandier would have you go to hell with him.

CLAIRE. So he gets the Devil to cry at night and break your heart, makes you put a rope round your neck, and hang yourself. Don't be deceived.

JEANNE. Is there no way? And is that Claire speaking? Claire, who used to talk to me of the innocence of Christ? What's the time?

GABRIELLE. Just past noon.

JEANNE. Let me stay here. I promise not to harm myself. Leave me.

(CLAIRE, LOUISE *and* GABRIELLE *exit* L.

JEANNE *crosses and sits on the stool, down* L. *The* LIGHTS *come up on the cell and area up* C *and* BLACK-OUT *on the area down* L, *except for a spotlight on Jeanne. The* LIGHTS *on the area down* R *dim to a low level.*

Two SOLDIERS *enter up* R *carrying a litter on which is the torture box; movable boards within the box, driven inwards by huge wedges, crush the legs of anyone in it. Lying on the box is a large mallet.* BONTEMPS *follows the Soldiers on, carrying a box of wedges. The* SOLDIERS *set the litter* C *up stage of the grille.* BONTEMPS *puts the box of wedges on the floor* R *of the litter.*

BARRÉ *and* RANGIER *enter* R. RANGIER *stands up* R *of the litter,* BARRE *stands* L *of it.* LAUBARDEMONT *and the* CAPTAIN *enter* R. LAUBARDEMONT *stands* R *of the litter. The* CAPTAIN *takes the keys from Bontemps, goes to the cell gate, unlocks and opens it.*

MANNOURY, ADAM *and* MIGNON *enter down* R. *They are presumed to be in another room.* MIGNON *and* MANNOURY *sit on the bench.* ADAM *paces restlessly,* JEANNE *remains seated down* L *in the convent garden.*

The CAPTAIN *ushers* GRANDIER *from the cell. A* SOLDIER *takes a wedge from the box and puts it in a slot*)

BARRÉ (*to Grandier*) Will you confess?

GRANDIER. No.

(BARRÉ *looks at* LAUBARDEMONT *who indicates for Grandier to be put in the box. The* SOLDIERS *put* GRANDIER *in the box, his head* L. *The* LIGHTS *up* C *are dimmed to a low level.* BONTEMPS *hammers the wedge home.* GRANDIER *screams.* JEANNE *reacts to each scream.* MIGNON *drops to his knees and prays*)

MANNOURY. What's the cubic capacity of a man's breath?
ADAM. Don't know.
MANNOURY. Just wondered.
ADAM. It doesn't occur to you when you start something, that . . . Hm!
MANNOURY. What did you say?
ADAM. Nothing. Just thinking aloud.
BARRÉ (*leans forward; to Grandier*) Confess.
GRANDIER. I'm only too ready to confess my real sins. I have been a man, I have loved women. I have longed for power.
BARRÉ. That's not what we want. You've been a magician. You've had commerce with devils.
GRANDIER. No. No.
BARRÉ. Another.

(*The* SOLDIER *takes a wedge from the box*)

Oh, give it to me. (*He snatches the wedge and places it in a slot*)

(BONTEMPS *hammers the wedge.* GRANDIER *screams.* JEANNE *reacts*)

JEANNE. Is it only in the very depths that one finds God? Look at me. First I wanted to come to Him in innocence. It was not enough. Then there was the lying and play-acting. The guilt, the humiliation. It was not enough. There were the antics done for the dirty eyes of priests. The squalor. It was not enough. Down, down further.

(*Another wedge is inserted.* BONTEMPS *hammers.* GRANDIER *screams*)

GRANDIER. God. God. God. Don't abandon me. Don't let this pain make me forget You.
JEANNE. Down. Down. Into idiot oblivion. No thought. No feeling. Nothing.

(*Another wedge is inserted.* BONTEMPS *hammers.* GRANDIER *screams*)

Is God here?
LAUBARDEMONT. Take him out.

(BARRÉ *crosses to Laubardemont*)

It's no good.

(*During the following conversation the* LIGHTS *up* C *come up to full.* BONTEMPS *lifts* GRANDIER *from the box and covers his shattered legs with a blanket. The* SOLDIERS *take the box from the litter, set the litter in the cell, then exit* R *with the box, wedges and mallet.*

BONTEMPS *carries Grandier into the cell and sits him on the litter, then exits* R.

The CAPTAIN *exits* R.

(BARRÉ *and* RANGIER *move down* R)

ADAM (*to Barré*) Any good?
BARRÉ. No.
MANNOURY. No confession?
BARRÉ. No.
ADAM. I say!
BARRÉ. Perfectly good reason.
MANNOURY. What?
BARRÉ. He called on God to give him strength. His God is the Devil and did so. Made him insensible to pain.

(BARRÉ, RANGIER *and* MIGNON *exit down* R.
ADAM *and* MANNOURY *exit* R)

JEANNE. Is God here?
GRANDIER. Behold and see if there is sorrow like unto my sorrow.
JEANNE (*rising*) Where are You? Where are You?

(JEANNE *exits* L.
The LIGHTS *dim to* BLACK-OUT *except on the area of the cell.*
LAUBARDEMONT *comes into the cell and stands up* L *of Grandier*)

GRANDIER. Take no notice of these tears. They're only weakness.
LAUBARDEMONT. Remorse?
GRANDIER. No.
LAUBARDEMONT. Confess.
GRANDIER. No.
LAUBARDEMONT. There are six thousand Christian souls waiting for you in the market-place. Tell me, do you love the Church?
GRANDIER. With all my heart.
LAUBARDEMONT. Do you want to see it grow more powerful, more benevolent, until it embraces every human soul on this earth?
GRANDIER. That would be my wish.
LAUBARDEMONT (*crossing above Grandier to* R *of him*) Then help us to achieve this great purpose. Go to the market-place a penitent man. Confess and by confessing, proclaim to those thousands that you have returned to the Church's arms. By going to the stake unrepentant you do God a disservice. You give hope to the sceptics and unbelievers. You make them glad. Such an act can mine the very foundations of the Church. (*He crosses above Grandier to* L *of him*) Think. You are no longer important. Are you any longer important?
GRANDIER. No.
LAUBARDEMONT. Then make a last supreme gesture for the Catholic faith.

(*There is a pause.* LAUBARDEMONT *eagerly leans forward, then* GRANDIER *looks up. His face is drawn in an agonized smile*)

GRANDIER. This is Sophistry, Laubardemont, and you're too intelligent not to know it. Pay me the same compliment.
LAUBARDEMONT. When I tell you, Grandier . . .

GRANDIER. Don't persist. I can destroy you. Keep your illusions. You'll need them all to deal with the men who will come after me.
LAUBARDEMONT. Confess.
GRANDIER. No.
LAUBARDEMONT. Confess. Confess.
GRANDIER. No.
LAUBARDEMONT. Sign.
GRANDIER (*shouting*) No.

(LAUBARDEMONT *goes to the cell gate*)

LAUBARDEMONT (*calling*) Let me have the guard here.

(*The* CLERK *enters* L *carrying a rope and a candle. He puts the rope around Grandier's neck and hands him the candle.* BONTEMPS *and two* SOLDIERS *enter* R, *come into the cell and lift the litter with Grandier on it. The grille is flown. The* LIGHTS *come up to full on the areas* C *down* R *and down* L.

Two DRUMMER BOYS, *the* CAPTAIN, BARRÉ, *four* SOLDIERS, RANGIER *and* MIGNON *enter* R. MIGNON *has a vessel of holy water. A procession is formed and moves anti-clockwise around the stage. The* CAPTAIN *leads, followed by the* DRUMMER BOYS, *then* BARRÉ, *the four* SOLDIERS, *the* CLERK, LAUBARDEMONT, RANGIER *and* MIGNON. MIGNON *sprinkles water as he goes. Finally comes* GRANDIER *on the litter, carried by* BONTEMPS *and two* SOLDIERS. GRANDIER'S *broken legs dangle. He is a ridiculous, hairless, shattered doll. As* BARRÉ *arrives down* L *and crosses to* R *he addresses the audience*)

BARRÉ. My dear children, you are about to witness the passage of a wicked and unrepentant man to hell. I beg of you—you, sir—take the sight to your heart. Let it be a lesson that will stay with you—my good woman—all your life. Watch this infamous magician who has trafficked with devils and ask yourself—my child—is that what a man comes to when he scorns God?

(*The* LIGHTS *come up on the bridge.*

JEANNE *enters* R *on the bridge and moves to* C *of it. The other* NUNS *enter and group* L *on the bridge. When the litter reaches the foot of the steps up* C *the procession halts as at St Ursula's Convent*)

LAUBARDEMONT (*to Grandier*) You must get down here.
GRANDIER. What is this place?
LAUBARDEMONT. It is the Convent of St Ursula. A place you have defiled. Do what must be done.
GRANDIER. In this strange and unknown place I ask pardon of God, the King and Justice. I beg that I may . . .

(*The* BEARERS *tip* GRANDIER *out of the litter. He falls full length on his back*)

Deus meus, miserere mei Deus.

LAUBARDEMONT. Ask pardon of this Prioress, and these good Sisters.

GRANDIER. Who are these women?

LAUBARDEMONT. They are the people you have wronged. Ask their forgiveness.

GRANDIER. I have done no such thing. I can only ask that God will forgive them.

(*There is a silence.* JEANNE *comes down the steps and stands above Grandier. She and* GRANDIER *stare at each other*)

JEANNE (*after a pause*) They always spoke of your beauty. Now I see it with my own eyes and I know it to be true.

GRANDIER. Look at this thing which I am, and learn the meaning of love.

(GRANDIER *is lifted on to the litter, the procession circles the stage.* MONKS *are heard chanting*)

MONKS (*chanting*) *Dies irae, dies illa, solvet seaclum in favilla, teste David Cum Sybilla. Quantus tremor est futurus, quando judex est venturus, cuncta stricte discussurus. Tuba minum spongeus sonus per sepulcha negionum oaget omnes ante thronum.*

(*A gong sounds. The* PROCESSION *exits* R.
    The NUNS *exit* L *on the bridge.*
    JEANNE *remains alone* C. *The* LIGHT *on the bridge and on the area* C *dim for night effect. There is a pause.*
    MANNOURY *and* ADAM *enter* R *on the bridge and cross to* C *of it*)

MANNOURY. Very odd, you know.

ADAM. What?

MANNOURY. That business of human fat being rendered down by heat to the consistency of candle wax and then igniting with a flame of such exquisite colour.

ADAM. Rum business, altogether.

MANNOURY. Interesting, though.

(ADAM *and* MANNOURY *cross and exit* L *on the bridge.*
    BARRÉ, MIGNON *and* RANGIER *enter* R *on the bridge and cross to* C *of it*)

BARRÉ. He's in hell. Be sure of it.

MIGNON. Tonight he roasts.

BARRÉ. Unrepentant, frightful man!

RANGIER. You know, I saw his women sitting there, watching. One was in tears, it's true, but she was watching. Never turned away.

BARRÉ. Devils. All devils.

(MIGNON *coughs*)

(*He turns to Mignon*) What's the matter with you?

MIGNON. I don't feel very well.

BARRÉ (*hitting* MIGNON *on the back*) Smoke got down you, I expect.

MIGNON. I think I'll go to bed now, if you don't mind.

(MIGNON *exits* L *on the bridge*)

BARRÉ (*following Mignon*) We're all going to get to our beds, Mignon. (*He stops and turns to Rangier*) How long we shall be allowed to lie there depends on friend Satan. We vanquished him and brought peace to this place today. But you can be sure that even now he is creeping back. (*He addresses the audience*) Ah, my dear friends, men of our kind will never lack employment.

(BARRÉ *and* RANGIER *exit* L *on the bridge.*
PHILLIPE *enters* R *on the bridge, leading an* OLD MAN *by the hand.*
PHILLIPE *is monstrously pregnant and lumbers forward*)

PHILLIPE. Come along home, dear husband. You must try to walk a little quicker.

(*The* OLD MAN *whispers to her*)

What?

(*The* OLD MAN *whispers*)

PHILLIPE. Watching all this today has made you quite excited.

(*The* OLD MAN *whispers*)

Yes, you shall do whatever you like. And I'll do all I can for you. Wipe your mouth. We've many happy years ahead together.

(PHILLIPE *and the* OLD MAN *exit* L *on the bridge.*
D'ARMAGNAC *and* DE CERISAY *enter* R *on the bridge. They are drunk*)

D'ARMAGNAC. We shouldn't be doing this, De Cerisay. We are the rational, forward-looking men of our age. We should be taking a stand. About something or other, I'm not quite sure what. Ask me tomorrow. Am I mad? Were they fornicating in the street up there? And what did that old woman have in the basket? Human remains? Why was that animal leading a man on a rope? What is the strange, sweet smell that hangs over the place? And that musician crucified upon the harp. What does it all mean, De Cerisay? As rational men we should be able to explain it.

DE CERISAY. I can't.

D'ARMAGNAC. Neither can I. So take me home.

(DE CERISAY *and* D'ARMAGNAC *exit* L *on the bridge.*
The LIGHTS *come up on the area* C.
A crowd of SOLDIERS *and* CITIZENS *enter* R *on the bridge, cross and exit* L. *They are fighting among themselves for some objects which are*

passed from hand to hand. Among them is the SEWERMAN. *He stops* C *on the bridge and addresses Jeanne)*

SEWERMAN. When it was done they shovelled him to the North, the South, the East and the West.

JEANNE. Do you know who I am?

SEWERMAN. Yes, madam, I know.

JEANNE (*indicating the Citizens*) What are they doing?

SEWERMAN. It's bits of the body they're after.

JEANNE. As relics?

SEWERMAN. Don't try to comfort yourself. No, they want them as charms. There's a difference, you know. (*He holds out a piece of charred bone*) They don't want to adore this. They want it to cure their constipation or their headache, to have it bring back their virility or their wife. They want it for love or hate. (*He tosses the bone to Jeanne*) Do you want it for anything?

(JEANNE *shakes her head. The* CROWD *has gone.*

The SEWERMAN *exits* L *on the bridge.*

JEANNE *is alone. The* LIGHTS BLACK-OUT *except for a spotlight on Jeanne)*

JEANNE (*crying out in her own voice*) Grandier! Grandier!

There is silence, then the spotlight on Jeanne dims to BLACK-OUT *as—*

the CURTAIN *falls*

FURNITURE AND PROPERTY LIST

ACT I

On stage: Corpse hanging on rope
In drain down C: bucket, spade
Bench (down R)
Table (down R)
Stool (down R)
Bench (down L)
Table (down L)
Stool (down L)

Off stage: 2 lanterns (FOOTMEN)
Sheaf of poems (TRINCANT)
Bottle of scent (NINON)
Human head in bucket with napkin cover (MANNOURY)
Mortar and pestle (ADAM)
Bishop's crozier (DE LA ROCHEPOZAY)
Carrying chairs (MONKS)
Ecclesiastical banner (ACOLYTES)
Smelling salts (DOCTOR)
Chair (SERVANT)

Sheaf of poems (SERVANT)
Sewing basket (SERVANT)
Stuffed crocodile and bladders (FLIES)
Shelves with bottles
Pieces of paper (ADAM)
Book (PHILLIPE)
Document (LOUIS)
Wicker ball (NUN)
Crutches (CRIPPLE BOYS)
Parchment and quill (LOUISE)
Inkstand (GABRIELLE)
Grubby document (DE LA ROCHEPOZAY)
Book (JEANNE)
Letter (CLAIRE)
2 candles (ACOLYTES)
Parchment and quill (MIGNON)

Personal: GRANDIER: handkerchief
DE LA ROCHEPOZAY: rings

ACT II

On stage: Benches, tables and stools down R and down L

Off stage: Bucket and spade (SEWERMAN)
Cage with bird (SEWERMAN)
Net (RANGIER)
Box with holy relic (MONK)
Container of holy water (MONK)
Copper kettle with boiling water (ADAM)
Bloodstained surgeon's apron (ADAM)
Copper bowl with dry ice (MANNOURY)
2 napkins (MANNOURY)
Clean surgeon's apron (MANNOURY)
Tray. *On it:* decanter of port, 3 glasses (SERVANT)
Litter with blanket (JEANNE)
Small table, stool, writing materials (CLERK)
Lantern (SERVANT)
Letter (D'ARMAGNAC)
Lantern (DE CERISAY)
Lantern (D'ARMAGNAC)
Pieces of paper (D'ARMAGNAC)
Relic box (PAGE)
Throne chair (SERVANT)
Banner (SERVANT)
Robes for Barre (MONK)

Ciborium (MONK)
Large jewelled cross (MONK)
Hand mirror (LOUISE)
Box (GRANDIER)
Bunch of flowers (GRANDIER)

Personal: GRANDIER: ring
DE CONDE: pomander

ACT III

On stage: Benches, tables and stools down R and down L
Bale of straw (C)
Grille with gate (C)

Off stage: Bucket of water (BONTEMPS)
Ladle (BONTEMPS)
Keys (BONTEMPS)
Books (AMBROSE)
Bag (ADAM)
Razor and strop (ADAM)
Tray. *On it:* bowl of water, empty silver cup, bottle of oil, small
    towel, make-up materials, bald eyebrows, spirit gum, mirror,
    bald pate (BONTEMPS)
Parchment (CLERK)
Gavel (CLERK)
Document (LAUBARDEMONT)
Quill (LAUBARDEMONT)
Rope (JEANNE)
Candle (JEANNE)
Cloak (LOUISE)
Litter. *On it:* torture box, mallet, blanket
Box of wedges (BONTEMPS)
Rope (CLERK)
2 drums (DRUMMER BOYS)
Vessel of holy water (MIGNON)
Relics (CROWD)
Charred bone (SEWERMAN)

LIGHTING PLOT

Property fittings required: candles

THE MAIN ACTING AREAS are on a bridge up C, C, down C, R, L, down R and down L. It should be arranged for these areas to be lit independently or collectively

ACT I

Cue 1   Before CURTAIN rises   (Page 1)
BLACK-OUT *onstage lights*

Cue 2   After rise of CURTAIN   (Page 1)
Bring up all lights for bright sunny daylight effect

Cue 3   GRANDIER and SEWERMAN exit   (Page 4)
Dim lights C for night effect
BLACK-OUT *surrounding areas*

Cue 4   D'ARMAGNAC and DE CERISAY exit   (Page 5)
BLACK-OUT *lights on area C*
Bring up lights on area down R

Cue 5   NINON exits   (Page 6)
BLACK-OUT *lights on area down R*
Bring up lights on area down L

Cue 6   MANNOURY and ADAM move C   (Page 6)
BLACK-OUT *lights on area down L*
Bring up lights on area C

Cue 7   MANNOURY and ADAM exit R   (Page 8)
BLACK-OUT *lights on area C*
Bring up shafts of light C to strike through stained glass window

Cue 8   GRANDIER: ". . . fons pietatis."   (Page 8)
BLACK-OUT *lights on window*
Bring up lights on areas down C, down RC and down LC

Cue 9   BARRÉ and RANGIER exit L   (Page 10)
BLACK-OUT *lights on areas C, RC, and LC*
Bring up lights on area down R

Cue 10   GRANDIER and Trincant exit   (Page 12)
BLACK-OUT *lights on area down R*
Bring up lights on area down L

Cue 11   ADAM: ". . . have a partner."   (Page 12)

BLACK-OUT *lights on area down* L
Bring in spotlight on area C

Cue 12   JEANNE: ". . . I must carry."   (Page 13)
Bring up lights on bridge

Cue 13   JEANNE: ". . . pots kept clean."   (Page 13)
Take out lights on bridge

Cue 14   JEANNE exits   (Page 13)
Take out spotlight
Bring in lights on area down R

Cue 15   PHILLIPE exits   (Page 14)
Take out lights on area down R
Bring in lights on centre of bridge
Bring in lights on Grandier down R

Cue 16   D'ARMAGNAC: ". . . can destroy you."   (Page 16)
Bring up lights on area C

Cue 17   RICHELIEU exits   (Page 16)
Take out lights down R
Bring up lights on the bridge and up C *to full*

Cue 18   JEANNE sits at table R   (Page 17)
All lights BLACK-OUT *except for a spotlight on Jeanne*

Cue 19   JEANNE: ". . . defence have You?"   (Page 18)
Bring up lights on bridge

Cue 20   ADAM and MANNOURY sit   (Page 18)
Take out spotlight on Jeanne

Cue 21   ADAM and MANNOURY exit   (Page 18)
Take out lights on bridge
Bring up lights on area down L

Cue 22   GRANDIER moves C   (Page 19)
Bring up lights on area C
Take out lights on area down L, *then* BLACK-OUT *as
Grandier and Phillipe exit* R

Cue 23   As DE LA ROCHEPOZAY enters   (Page 19)
Bring up lights on area C

Cue 24   DE LA ROCHEPOZAY exits   (Page 20)
Take out lights on area C
When scene set, bring up lights on area RC *and* C *for night
effect*

Cue 25   CLAIRE exits   (Page 21)
Dim all lights to BLACK-OUT *except for a spotlight on
Jeanne* C

Cue 26   JEANNE: "... be to Man."   (Page 21)
             Bring up dim light on right end of bridge. This holds for
                45 seconds, then fades out

Cue 27   JEANNE: "Is that it?"   (Page 21)
             BLACK-OUT *all lights*

Cue 28   When cloisters flown   (Page 21)
             Bring in lights on bridge and area C

Cue 29   D'ARMAGNAC: "... across our path."   (Page 22)
             BLACK-OUT. *When the scene set bring up lights on bridge*
                and area C

Cue 30   JEANNE and MIGNON move R   (Page 23)
             Bring up lights on area R
             Take out lights on area C

Cue 31   JEANNE: "Help me, Father."   (Page 24)
             Dim lights on area R
             Bring lights in on area C

Cue 32   GRANDIER exits   (Page 25)
             Take out lights on area C *and* R
             Bring up lights on area L

Cue 33   ADAM: "At last."   (Page 25)
              Dim lights on area L
              Bring up lights on area C *for night effect*

Cue 34   GRANDIER: "You shame me."   (Page 26)
             Take out lights on area C
              Bring up lights on area L

Cue 35   LAUBARDEMONT: "It'll soon be morning."   (Page 27)
             Dim lights on area L *to* BLACK-OUT
             Bring up lights on area R *for dawn effect*

Cue 36   JEANNE: "Amen."   (Page 27)
              Bring up general lighting to full for bright morning effect

Cue 37   JEANNE: "Grandier."   (Page 27)
             BLACK-OUT

ACT II

Cue 38   Before CURTAIN rises   (Page 28)
             BLACK-OUT *on stage lights*

Cue 39   After rise of CURTAIN   (Page 28)
             Bring up lights through stained glass window C

Cue 40   GRANDIER and PHILLIPE move R   (Page 28)
            Take out lights through window
            Bring up lights down C *for night effect*

Cue 41   GRANDIER and the SEWERMAN exit   (Page 30)
            Dim all lights to BLACK-OUT *when scene set bring up lights*
                C *for bright daylight effect*

Cue 42   JEANNE is taken off L   (Page 32)
            BLACK-OUT
            After scream, bring up lights on area down R

Cue 43   GRANDIER and D'ARMAGNAC exit   (Page 34)
            Take out lights on area down R
            Bring in lights on area C

Cue 44   JEANNE: "I have found peace."   (Page 36)
            Take out lights on area C
            Bring up lights on areas down R *and down* L

Cue 45   BARRÉ: "That's all I need."   (Page 37)
            Take out lights on areas down R *and down* L

Cue 46   PHILLIPE: "I'm pregnant."   (Page 38)
            Increase light on area C

Cue 47   GRANDIER and PHILLIPE exit   (Page 39)
            Take out lights on area C
            Bring in lights on area down L

Cue 48   BARRÉ: ". . . shall be back."   (Page 40)
            Take out lights on area down L
            Bring up lights on area down R

Cue 49   GRANDIER: "Forsaken."   (Page 41)
            Take out lights on area down R
            Bring up lights on area C *for bright daylight effect*

Cue 50   JEANNE: ". . . not the intention."   (Page 42)
            Take out lights on the area C
            Bring up lights on bridge for night effect

Cue 51   D'ARMAGNAC: "Let's go down."   (Page 42)
            Take out lights on bridge
            Bring in dim light on Grandier down R

Cue 52   GRANDIER exits R   (Page 43)
            Take out lights on area down R
            Bring in lights on area down L

Cue 53   LAUBARDEMONT: "Here and now."   (Page 43)
            Bring up lights on area C

Cue 54   LAUBARDEMONT: "Well done."   (Page 44)
            Bring up lights on bridge and on area down R

ACT III

Cue 71	CLAIRE: ". . . in that way?" *Take out lights on area down* R *Bring up lights on area* C	(Page 58)
Cue 72	GRANDIER kneels at tray *Take out lights on area* C *Bring in lights on areas down* R *and down* L	(Page 60)
Cue 73	CLERK: ". . . the same day." *Bring up lights* C	(Page 61)
Cue 74	GRANDIER returns to the cell *Take out lights* C	(Page 63)
Cue 75	D'ARMAGNAC and DE CERISAY exit *Bring up lights down* C *leaving the cell in shadow*	(Page 63)
Cue 76	JEANNE: "Leave me." *Bring up lights on cell and area up* C *Take out lights on area down* L *except for a spotlight on* *Jeanne* *Dim lights on area down* R *to a low level*	(Page 64)
Cue 77	GRANDIER is put in box *Reduce lights up*	(Page 64)
Cue 78	LAUBARDEMONT: "It's no good." *Bring up lights up* C	(Page 65)
Cue 79	JEANNE: "Where are You?" *All lights dim to* BLACK-OUT *except for the area of the cell*	(Page 66)
Cue 80	The grille is flown *Bring up lights to full on the areas* C, *down* R *and down* L	(Page 67)
Cue 81	BARRÉ: ". . . he scorns God." *Bring up lights on bridge*	(Page 67)
Cue 82	The PROCESSION exits *Dim all lights for night effect*	(Page 68)
Cue 83	DE CERISAY and D'ARMAGNAC exit *Bring up lights on area* C	(Page 69)
Cue 84	The SEWERMAN exits BLACK-OUT *all lights except for a spot on Jeanne*	(Page 70)
Cue 85	JEANNE: "Grandier! Grandier!" BLACK-OUT *spot on Jeanne*	(Page 70)

EFFECTS PLOT

ACT I

Cue 15	MIGNON runs around *Demoniac laughter*	(Page 48)
Cue 16	CLAIRE: "Yes." NUNS *in the distance singing Plainsong*	(Page 49)
Cue 17	LEVIATHAN: ". . . not even dignity." *singing ceases*	(Page 50)
Cue 18	JEANNE exits L *Sound of distant trumpet*	(Page 50)
Cue 19	RICHELIEU and LOUIS exit *Sound of church bells*	(Page 51)

ACT III

Cue 20	GRANDIER kneels at tray *Sound of large crowd murmuring*	(Page 60)
Cue 21	The CLERK raps with gavel *Sound of crowd fades*	(Page 60)
Cue 22	GRANDIER is pushed down C *Loud gasp of horror from crowd*	(Page 61)
Cue 23	GRANDIER: "Amen." *Crowd murmur "Amen"*	(Page 61)
Cue 24	GRANDIER: ". . . meaning of love." MONKS *chanting*	(Page 68)
Cue 25	At end of chanting *Sound of a gong*	(Page 68)

Character costumes and wigs used in the performance of plays contained in French's Acting Edition may be obtained from Messrs CHARLES H. FOX LTD, 184 High Holborn, London W.C.1.

MADE AND PRINTED IN GREAT BRITAIN BY
LATIMER TREND AND CO. LTD, WHITSTABLE
MADE IN ENGLAND